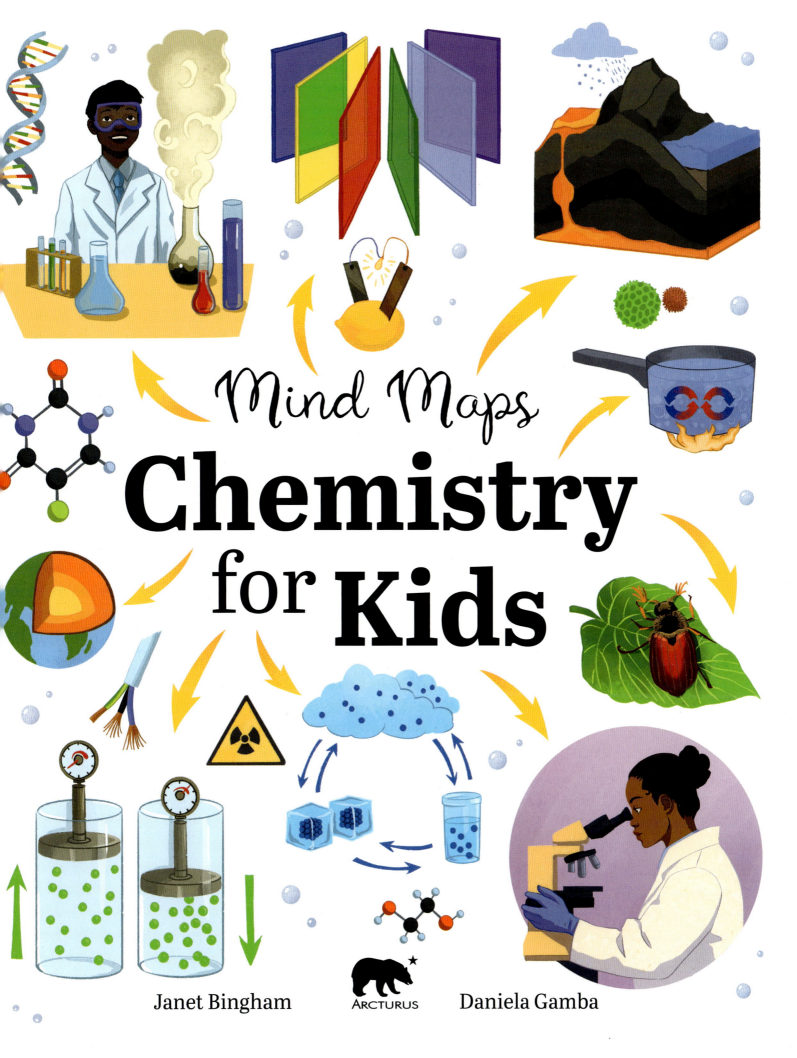

Mind Maps
Chemistry
for Kids

Janet Bingham

ARCTURUS

Daniela Gamba

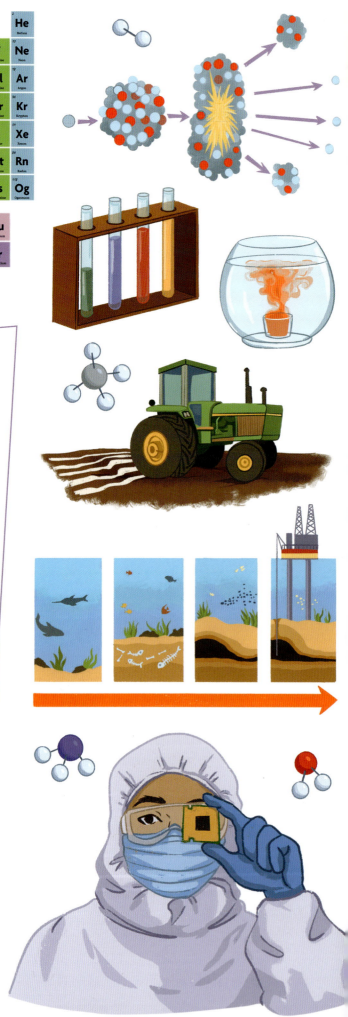

ARCTURUS

This edition published in 2025 by Arcturus Publishing Limited
26/27 Bickels Yard, 151–153 Bermondsey Street, London SW1 3HA

Author: Janet Bingham
Consultant: Anne Rooney
Illustrator: Daniela Gamba
Front cover illustrator: Anna Kuptsova
Designer: Sally Bond
Editor: Lydia Halliday
Editorial Manager: Joe Harris
Design Manager: Jessica Holliland

ISBN: 9781-3988-5064-4
CH011025US
Supplier 29, Date 0425, PI 00010281

Printed in China

How this book works

Nonliving and living things are all connected. If you are interested in how a candle burns, the topic links to many others, such as ...

Chemistry connects everything!

That's because everything is made of chemicals. All substances, from our own bodies to our electronic devices, are made of atoms—the tiny, invisible particles of chemicals that build all the matter in the Universe.

Why some chemical reactions give off energy

The symbols scientists use to describe chemicals and explain reactions

Hydrocarbon molecules and crude oil

Why a burning candle is like respiration in living cells

The invisible gases that make up Earth's atmosphere

How atoms make and break bonds to form molecules

Make the link ...

This book shows you how chemistry connects everything, by linking topics together in a big mind map. Whenever there's a connection to a related topic, you'll see a link, like this:

You can read the sections and topics in any order. Try looking for a topic that interests you, using the contents diagram on the next page. Then follow the page links to find out where the mind map can take you.

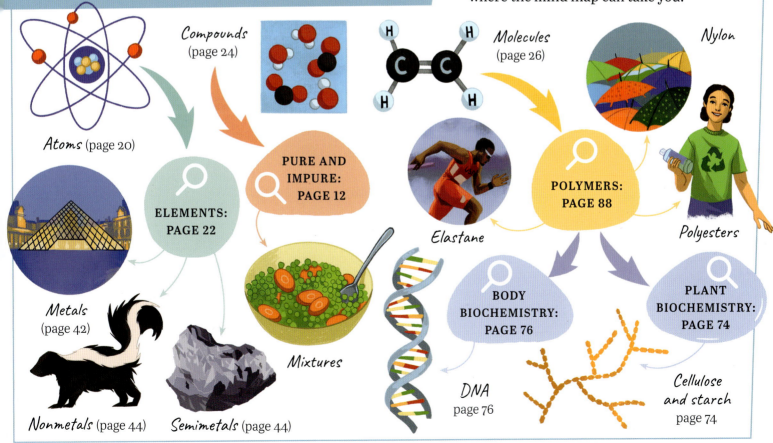

Atoms (page 20)

Compounds (page 24)

Molecules (page 26)

Nylon

PURE AND IMPURE: PAGE 12

ELEMENTS: PAGE 22

POLYMERS: PAGE 88

Elastane

Polyesters

Metals (page 42)

Mixtures

BODY BIOCHEMISTRY: PAGE 76

PLANT BIOCHEMISTRY: PAGE 74

Nonmetals (page 44)

Semimetals (page 44)

DNA page 76

Cellulose and starch page 74

What's in the book?

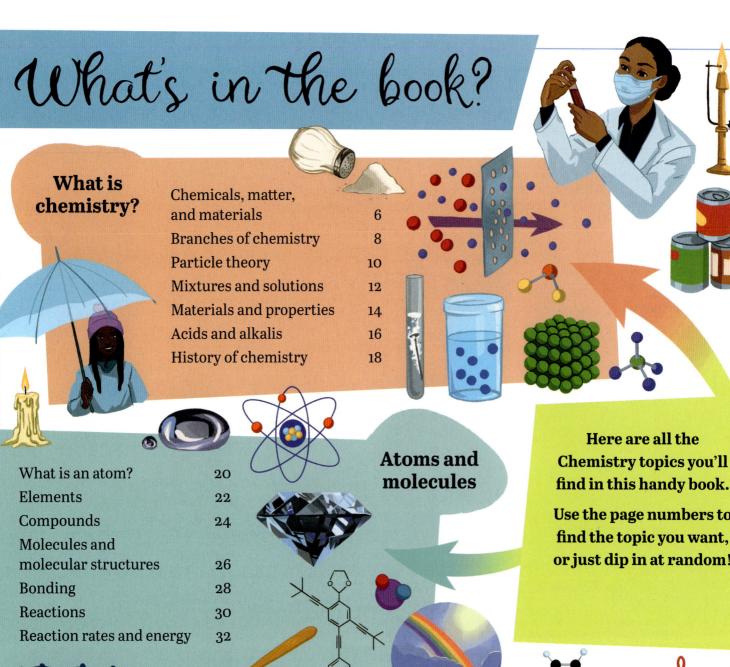

What is chemistry?

Atoms and molecules

Here are all the Chemistry topics you'll find in this handy book.

Use the page numbers to find the topic you want, or just dip in at random!

Elements and the Periodic Table

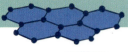

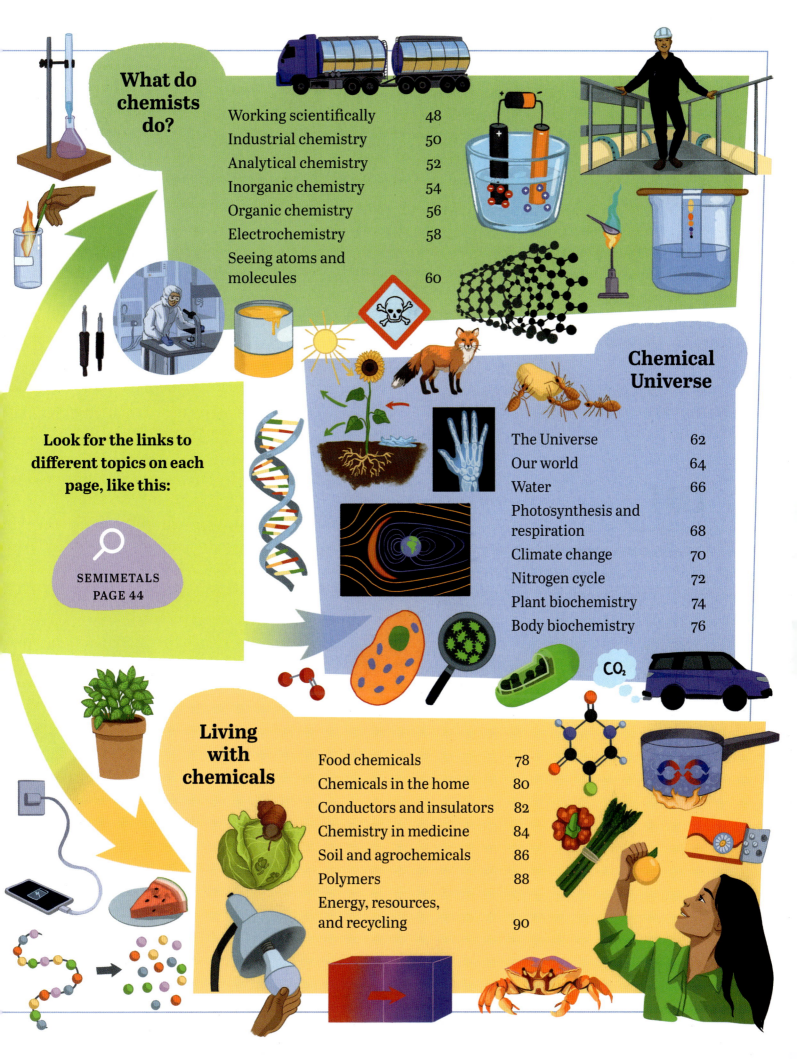

What do chemists do?

Look for the links to different topics on each page, like this:

SEMIMETALS
PAGE 44

Chemical Universe

Living with chemicals

Chemicals, matter, and materials

Chemistry is the science of chemicals. You may not have noticed chemicals, but you notice what they do. They make up everything you can see, touch, hear, or smell—all the matter in the Universe.

Matter is made up of millions of different chemicals. Just 118 chemicals are the simplest chemicals of all—elements. They are building blocks that team up to make everything else.

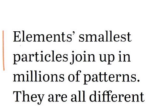

Elements' smallest particles join up in millions of patterns. They are all different chemicals.

ELEMENTS: PAGE 22

Matter makes different substances and materials through all the combinations of chemicals. The most amazing combinations make living things.

Chemicals make the matter in all the structures of the Universe. Anything that takes up space is matter. Even "empty" space contains some matter.

The Universe has billions of galaxies like our Milky Way.

MORE

THE UNIVERSE: PAGE 62

Finding chemicals

We can investigate chemicals everywhere.

... under a microscope.

... through a telescope.

... in laboratory equipment.

We all use chemicals in the kitchen.

States of Matter

Matter can be liquids, solids, or gases. These are the "states of matter." As matter gets warmer or colder, it changes from one state to another.

Earth is just the right temperature to have water in liquid, solid, and gas form.

Our world has liquid water, ice, and water vapor in the air.

🔍 CHANGING STATES: PAGE 11

Mixtures and solutions

Chemicals in liquids, solids, and gases jumble up to make mixtures and solutions.

Air is a mixture of gases.

Sweet tea is a solution of sugar and tea.

🔍 MIXTURES AND SOLUTIONS: PAGE 12

🔍 COMPOUNDS: PAGE 24

Compounds

A chemical reaction is when chemicals combine by bonding. It makes new, different chemicals called compounds. Chemists control chemical reactions to create new materials, with new uses.

Water is a compound made of two gases— hydrogen and oxygen.

Substances and materials

A substance is anything made of matter. Materials are substances with useful properties. Metals, plastics, paper, and wood are examples of materials.

Plastic bottle

Metal cans

Sheets of paper

A wooden shed

🔍 MATERIALS: PAGE 14

Living things

Life is possible because of "organic chemicals"— chemicals that contain carbon and hydrogen and a few other important elements.

Plants use the Sun's energy to make organic chemicals to build their bodies.

The chemicals pass through the food chain.

In nature, chemicals are recycled from plant and animal waste.

🔍 DECOMPOSITION: PAGE 73

🔍 PHOTOSYNTHESIS: PAGE 68

🔍 FOOD CHAINS: PAGE 68

Branches of chemistry

Chemists study chemicals to explore why they look and behave as they do. The different branches of chemistry look at the subject from different directions. The branches often overlap and twist together.

Everything is made of chemicals, so the branches of chemistry connect with other sciences, from biology to astronomy. Studying chemicals in plants helps explain how things are alive. Studying chemicals in rocks can explain how Earth formed.

Two of the branches of chemistry relate to two big groups—organic and inorganic chemicals. Other branches are to do with the different ways chemists study chemicals, or with the different uses of the chemicals.

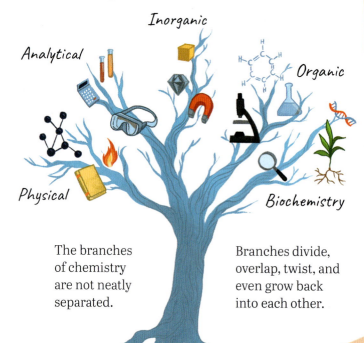

Inorganic

Analytical

Organic

Physical

Biochemistry

The branches of chemistry are not neatly separated.

Branches divide, overlap, twist, and even grow back into each other.

The main branches of chemistry are:

- Physical
- Analytical
- Inorganic
- Organic
- Biochemistry
- Materials
- Chemical engineering
- Theoretical chemistry

Physical

Physical chemists look at how substances behave, and measure how they change in chemical reactions. What are the rules chemicals follow when they interact, react, and transform into new substances?

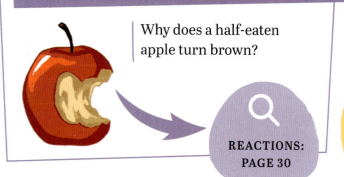

Why does a half-eaten apple turn brown?

REACTIONS: PAGE 30

Analytical

Analytical chemistry is about doing experiments to find out what chemicals—and how much of them—a substance contains.

How do you discover what's in the test tube?

ANALYTICAL CHEMISTRY: PAGE 52

Inorganic

Compounds that don't contain carbon and hydrogen are inorganic chemicals. Inorganic chemistry includes metals, minerals, and ceramics.

INORGANIC CHEMISTRY: PAGE 54

How do we make glass from sand?

Organic

Carbon reacts with hydrogen and a few other elements to make organic chemicals. Fossil fuels (oil, gas, and coal) and polymers (plastics) are organic.

The bodies of living things are made of organic chemicals.

ORGANIC CHEMISTRY: PAGE 56

Biochemistry

Biochemistry is biological chemistry. Biochemists study chemicals and chemical processes in living things.

How does a tree use energy from the sun to grow?

PLANT BIOCHEMISTRY: PAGE 74

Materials

Materials chemists are interested in the properties of raw materials, synthetic and natural materials, and exciting new smart materials. They find applications (jobs) for materials.

MATERIALS CHEMIST: PAGE 49

Double-glazed windows contain argon.

Theoretical

Theoretical chemistry uses math and computers to explain the laws that control the structure and behavior of chemicals. A theoretical chemist might predict a chemical reaction before it's been done as an experiment.

Chemical engineering

Chemical engineering is using chemical processes and equipment to manufacture (make) industrial products.

INDUSTRIAL CHEMISTRY: PAGE 50

Particle theory

Particle theory explains why a solid keeps its shape, liquids flow through your fingers, and gas escapes in all directions. It's because the tiny particles are arranged differently in different states.

Matter is made of tiny particles—atoms and molecules. In particle theory, we think of atoms and molecules as simple balls. The particles move. They vibrate (jiggle), and sometimes they whiz around. When they gain energy, they move faster.

WHAT IS AN ATOM: PAGE 20

Solid   Liquid   Gas

The particles give solids, liquids, and gases their properties:

- Shape
- Flow
- Mass (amount)
- Volume (the space it fills)
- Density (heaviness)
- Compressibility (squashiness)

Solids

Solids have a definite volume and density, and they can't be squashed. The particles are held close together and can only vibrate.

A solid's particles aren't pushed closer, even when you squeeze it.

Liquids

Liquids change shape and flow. A liquid can't be stretched or be squashed. It has a definite volume and density.

The particles move past each other.

MATERIALS AND PROPERTIES: PAGE 14

Liquids flow into the shape of a container.

Gases

Gases flow and expand into all the space they can—they diffuse. The mass of gas stays the same, but its volume and density change. Gases can be squashed.

Pumping up a bicycle tire squashes air into the space.

Changing states

Matter changes state when the temperature changes. Changes of state are reversible physical changes—they can change back.

WATER:
PAGE 66

When a solid heats up, the particles gain energy and vibrate more. With enough energy, they start moving past each other. The solid melts and becomes liquid.

Evaporation is liquid becoming vapor—changing into gas. Particles on a liquid's surface are always escaping. It happens faster as they heat up and get more energy.

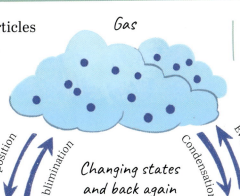

Gas

Deposition

Sublimation

Condensation

Evaporation

Changing states and back again

Solid

Liquid

Freezing

Melting

ENERGY:
PAGE 32

Freezing and melting point temperatures are the same. Ice melts and water freezes at 0 °C (32 °F).

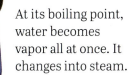

Water boils at 100 °C (212 °F). Other liquids boil at different temperatures.

At its boiling point, water becomes vapor all at once. It changes into steam.

When steam cools, it condenses into liquid.

Brownian motion

The particles inside liquids and gases move in all directions and bounce off each other. This random movement of particles is Brownian motion.

Liquid particles diffuse through other liquids by Brownian motion.

Food dye spreads in water.

MIXTURES AND
SOLUTIONS:
PAGE 12

Boyle's law

A gas can be squashed into a smaller space because the pressure pushes the particles closer together.

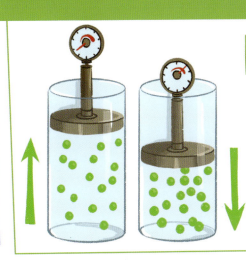

A gas's volume gets smaller as the pressure increases. This is Boyle's law.

Mixtures and solutions

When you mix peas and potato on your plate, you make a mixture of vegetables. The ingredients are physically mixed up, but they don't change. Solids, liquids, and gases mix together to make mixtures and solutions.

Mixed solids are mixtures. Liquids and liquids make solutions. Liquids with gases or solids dissolved in them are also solutions. Mixtures and solutions can be separated, but not always easily.

Air is a mixture of nitrogen, oxygen, carbon dioxide, and other gases.

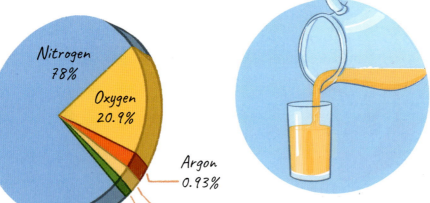

Nitrogen 78%

Oxygen 20.9%

Argon 0.93%

Other gases 0.13%

Carbon dioxide 0.04%

Orange juice is a solution of juice and water.

Particles in mixtures and solutions are not chemically joined, so they can be separated by physical processes.

MORE

Pure and Impure

Mixtures and solutions are impure—they contain more than one substance. A pure substance contains only one kind of thing—whether it's vegetables, molecules,* or atoms.

Carrots with peas is a mixture. Picking the peas out leaves pure carrots.

Dissolving

Salt is soluble. It breaks up into smaller particles and dissolves in water. You can't see it, but you can taste it. The salt in the solution is the "solute," and the water is the "solvent."

COMPOUNDS: PAGE 24

Concentration

Concentration is how much stuff is dissolved. A solution of a little sugar in water is dilute. Adding more sugar makes it more concentrated.

Dye solutions get paler as they get more dilute.

*Molecules are the smallest particles of compounds.

Separating solids from solids

Sieving: The holes in a sieve let small particles through and catch bigger particles.

People sieve gold out of river mud.

Magnetism: Magnets attract iron-based metals.

In recycling, magnets sort waste steel from aluminum.

MAGNETS: PAGE 42

Separating solids from liquids

Filtering: A filter catches solids and lets liquids through.

We strain coffee through the small holes in filter paper.

Evaporation: Dissolved solids are separated from solutions by evaporation.

Salt is gathered from evaporating lakes.

CHANGING STATES: PAGE 11

Separating liquids from liquids

Distillation: A solution of liquids can be separated by heating until one evaporates, leaving the other behind.

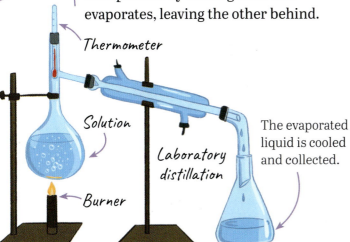

Thermometer

Solution

Burner

Laboratory distillation

The evaporated liquid is cooled and collected.

Fractional distillation: Crude oil contains many substances (fractions) used as fuels and chemicals. They evaporate at different temperatures.

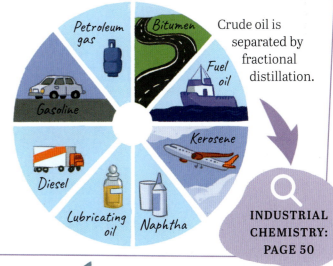

Petroleum gas

Bitumen

Fuel oil

Gasoline

Kerosene

Diesel

Lubricating oil

Naphtha

Crude oil is separated by fractional distillation.

INDUSTRIAL CHEMISTRY: PAGE 50

Separating molecules

Molecular sieves: Materials with very tiny pores (holes) separate the particles in gases or liquids. A molecular sieve lets through tiny hydrogen and catches larger gas particles.

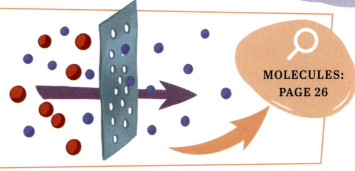

MOLECULES: PAGE 26

Materials and properties

People have used materials since they first poked a stick into an anthill to search for ants. Wood naturally has useful properties—it's hard, light, and quite stiff. Other materials are made or processed to make them useful.

Metals, plastics, ceramics, wood, paper, and fabrics are examples of materials. We choose the material with the best properties for a job. Bricks are ceramic. They're heat-resistant, and don't dissolve in the rain. That's why we build houses with bricks ...

... and not gingerbread

Natural and Synthetic

Natural materials are materials from the Earth or living things, such as coal or wood. Synthetic materials are designed to do jobs better. Synthetic nylon is stronger than natural cotton, so it makes longer-lasting clothes.

It's important to recycle all the plastics we use.

POLYMERS: PAGE 88

Plastics are synthetic polymers. They have many different forms and properties. They are versatile—do many jobs—and we use them everywhere.

Raw materials

Materials are made from raw materials. Crude oil is a raw material. It's separated and processed into fuels and chemicals used to make plastics.

FRACTIONAL DISTILLATION: PAGE 50

FOSSIL FUELS: PAGE 90

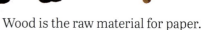

Wood is the raw material for paper.

Some properties are:
- Conducting/insulating
- Hard/soft
- Heavy/light
- Malleable/brittle
- Permeable/impermeable
- Rough/smooth
- Soluble/insoluble
- Transparent/opaque

Improved Materials

Composites combine materials to improve their properties.

Kayaks are fiberglass—light plastic strengthened with glass fibers.

COMPOSITES: PAGE 80

NANO-TECHNOLOGY: PAGE 60

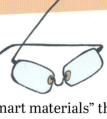

Smart Materials

Scientists are creating "smart materials" that change themselves. Bent eyeglasses frames made of shape-memory alloys spring back into shape when heated. Nanomaterials (tiny particles) keep room temperatures steady. Smart materials are getting smarter!

Conducting/insulating

Conductors let heat or electricity pass through. Nonconducting materials are insulating.

A metal pan conducts heat. Plastic insulates the handle.

CONDUCTORS AND INSULATORS: PAGE 82

Hard/soft

We use strong, hard materials for tough jobs.

A hammer and nails are made of steel.

Soft foams are better for sofas!

Heavy/light

Metals are heavier than nonmetals. Coins sink, but wood is light enough to float.

A ship floats because the air inside it is lighter than water.

DENSITY: PAGE 10

Malleable/brittle

Metals are flexible—they're malleable and ductile (can be shaped and drawn into wires).

Nonmetals like china are brittle—they break easily.

METALS: PAGE 42

Permeable/impermeable

Permeable things let water soak through.

Umbrellas are impermeable—they're waterproof.

Rough/smooth

Polished metals are smooth, shiny, and reflect light. Nonmetals are often rough, dull, and nonreflective.

Coal looks dull in a shiny copper bucket.

NONMETALS: PAGE 44

Transparent/opaque

Window glass is transparent—see-through.

Soluble/insoluble

Soluble pills dissolve in water.

The glass is insoluble.

DISSOLVING: PAGE 12

Curtains are opaque to block out the light.

Acids and alkalis

Many household substances are acids or alkalis. Car batteries contain sulfuric acid. Vinegar is acetic acid. Bleach is an alkali. Pure water is neutral—not acid or alkali.

Chemicals dissolve to make solutions that are acidic, alkaline (basic), or neutral. Acids and alkalis are corrosive—they "eat away" substances. They can be strong or weak. Strong acids and alkalis can burn skin, damage materials, and even attack metals!

WORKING SAFELY: PAGE 48

DISSOLVING: PAGE 12

Neutral solutions are pH 7.

pH

The pH scale measures how strong acids and alkalis are. Acids score between pH 0 and pH 6, and pH 0 is the strongest. Alkalis score between pH 8 and pH 14, and pH 14 is the strongest.

Some acids and alkalis are found in:

- Your stomach
- Fruit
- Rainwater
- Baking soda
- Cleaning chemicals

Universal indicator can be dipping paper or a liquid in the test solution.

Indicators

Litmus paper turns red when dipped into acids and turns blue in alkalis.

Universal indicator shows the strength of an alkali or acid by changing color to match a shade on the pH scale.

Concentration

A concentrated solution contains a lot of acid (or alkali). Adding more water makes it more dilute. A concentrated strong acid is very hazardous. Diluting fruit juice makes it better for your teeth.

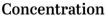

Workers with concentrated strong acids use protective clothing.

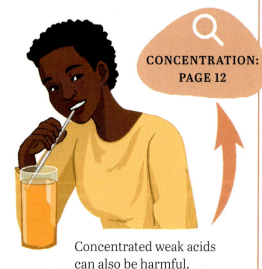

CONCENTRATION: PAGE 12

Concentrated weak acids can also be harmful.

Your stomach

You digest your food with hydrochloric acid. Stomach acid can be as high as pH 1 and can cause indigestion — called "heartburn" because it feels like fire!

Alkali "antacids" neutralize stomach acid.

CHEMISTRY IN MEDICINE: PAGE 84

Fruit

Citrus fruits are rich in ascorbic acid—vitamin C. Citric acid makes lemons taste sour. Apples contain malic acid.

It is better for your teeth to eat fruit at mealtimes rather than between meals.

FOOD CHEMICALS: PAGE 78

Rainwater

Rainwater is around pH 6. Sulfur dioxide pollution makes it more acidic. Acid rain can dissolve stone.

CLIMATE CHANGE: PAGE 70

Baking soda

Baking soda is sodium bicarbonate, a weak alkali.

Baking soda is used in cooking and cleaning.

BAKING SODA

Cleaning chemicals

Oven and drain cleaners contain sodium hydroxide, a strong alkali.

Sodium hydroxide is caustic soda.

SODIUM HYDROXIDE: PAGE 51

Reactions

Neutralization

Acids and alkalis neutralize each other. They react to form water and a neutral compound called a "salt." There are many different salts.

Farmers neutralize acid soils with calcium oxide.

Acids and metal oxides

Metal oxides such as iron oxide (rust) make alkaline solutions. So, metal oxides neutralize acids.

Copper sulfate, a fungicidal salt, is made by the neutralization of copper oxide with sulfuric acid.

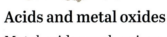

Sodium chloride (table salt) is made by hydrochloric acid reacting with sodium hydroxide.

Acids and metals

Acids react with metals to make a salt and hydrogen.

An iron nail in hydrochloric acid makes bubbles of hydrogen gas.

REACTIONS: PAGE 30

17

History of chemistry

We love questions. Why is the sea salty? What makes the sun shine? Can I eat this? Over the ages, our natural curiosity has turned into modern science—the careful study of the world.

Chemistry goes back to early herbalists and healers who discovered that plants could made sick people better or healthy people sick. People who discovered how to improve metals by mixing them into alloys over 4,000 years ago were doing chemistry.

Mixing tin and copper began in the Bronze Age.

METALS: PAGE 42

Historical breakthroughs in modern chemistry have been moments of genius, discovery, and invention, such as:

- Defining elements
- Nomenclature
- The battery
- Atomic theory
- Radioactivity
- The spectroscope
- Periodic Table
- Atomic structure

Deep thinking

The philosophers of the ancient world were the first "deep thinkers." They wanted to know what matter was made of, as long ago as 500 BCE. Greek philosophers like Aristotle believed in four "elements"—earth, air, fire, and water—that made up everything.

Aristotle
(384–322 BCE)

MORE

Alchemy

Alchemy began in Egypt and Arabia, spreading to Greece and the rest of Europe. Alchemists added mercury, sulfur, and salt to the philosophers' list of "elements."

Medieval alchemists searched for the "Philosopher's Stone," hoping to turn ordinary metals like lead into gold. They also believed the Stone could help people live forever.

Alchemists developed experimental methods and equipment. Instead of the Stone, they discovered many real elements and useful compounds.

In 1669, Hennig Brand discovered phosphorus in urine (pee).

Alchemy eventually became modern chemistry.

Defining elements

In 1661, Robert Boyle defined an element as something that couldn't be broken down into a simpler substance.

Gold is an element.

ELEMENTS: PAGE 22

Nomenclature

In 1789, Antoine Lavoisier introduced a way of naming compounds that we still use.

Lavoisier's wife worked with him.

The battery

In 1800, Alessandro Volta invented the battery.

Humphrey Davy used it to discover elements by electrolysis.

ELECTRO-CHEMISTRY: PAGE 58

Atomic theory

In 1803, John Dalton stated that atoms of one element are alike and different to atoms of other elements.

Dalton realized chemical reactions rearranged the atoms.

Hydrogen   Oxygen   Water

Water is made of hydrogen and oxygen.

WHAT IS AN ATOM?: PAGE 20

Radioactivity

In 1896, Henri Becquerel discovered radioactivity.

 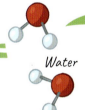

He found that uranium left an image on photographic film.

THE HEAVIEST ELEMENTS: PAGE 46

The spectroscope

In 1859, Robert Bunsen and Gustav Kirchhoff invented the spectroscope to separate the colors in light.

Many elements have been discovered with the spectroscope.

SPECTROSCOPY: PAGE 53

Atomic structure

In 1911, Ernest Rutherford showed that atoms are mostly empty space around a central nucleus.

He fired tiny particles at thin gold leaf and found that some of them bounced back.

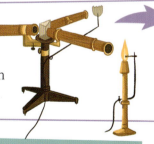

SEEING ATOMS AND MOLECULES: PAGE 60

Periodic Table

In 1869, Dmitry Mendeleyev organized the elements by mass.

Mendeleyev's system led to our modern Periodic Table.

ORGANIZING ELEMENTS: PAGE 34

What is an atom?

Atoms are tiny particles that make up all matter. It's sometimes useful to think of them as simple balls, but they're more interesting than that. Atoms are made up of even smaller—subatomic—particles.

Elements—the simplest chemicals—contain just one kind of atom. Imagine if a magic knife could cut tinier and tinier crumbs of an element.

ELEMENTS: PAGE 22

The tiniest crumb the magic knife could cut would be an atom.*

THE UNIVERSE: PAGE 62

Subatomic particles—protons, neutrons, and electrons—give elements their properties.

Atomic structure

The atoms of one element are different to other atoms. The number of subatomic particles makes the difference.

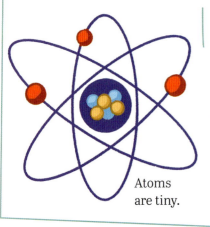

Atoms are tiny.

An atom has a central nucleus** containing protons and neutrons. Electrons move around the nucleus like planets around a sun.

The radius may be just 0.1 nm (0.0000001 mm)—and they are mostly empty space.

An atom as big as an American football stadium would have a nucleus like a pea in the middle, with electrons whizzing all around the stadium.

Atomic radius

*Most atoms except hydrogen are created in the stars.
**The plural of nucleus is nuclei.

MORE

Electron shells

Equal and opposite charges of the nucleus and electrons produce an electromagnetic force. This holds the electrons close to the nucleus in areas called electron shells.

The shells are stacked inside each other like Russian dolls, but they're not solid.

As the atoms in the Periodic Table get bigger, they get more electrons and more shells.

PERIODIC TABLE: PAGES 36–37

Electrons in the outer shells create the bonds that connect atoms inside molecules.

BONDING: PAGE 28

Protons

Protons* have mass (weight). Protons are positive, which makes the nucleus positive.

The number of protons in one atom is that element's atomic number.

Lithium has 3 protons and 4 neutrons.

Lithium is so light, it floats on oil.

ELEMENT GROUP 1: PAGE 41

*Protons and neutrons together make the nucleus "massive"—it has mass.

Neutrons

Neutrons have mass. One neutron weighs about the same as a proton. Neutrons are neutral—they have no charge.

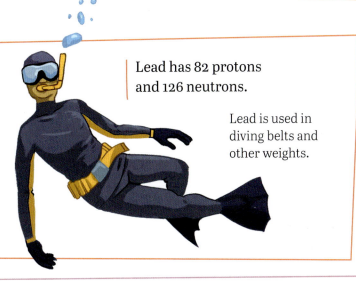

Lead has 82 protons and 126 neutrons.

Lead is used in diving belts and other weights.

Electrons

An electron has lots of energy, but almost no mass—it's 2,000 times lighter than a proton. Electrons have a negative charge.

An atom has the same number of electrons as protons. The negative and positive charges balance—so a whole atom has no charge. An atom that has lost or gained an electron is an "ion."

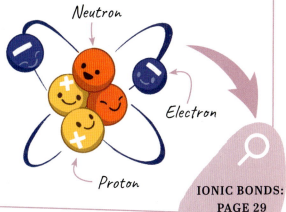

Neutron

Electron

Proton

IONIC BONDS: PAGE 29

Isotopes

Isotopes are forms of an element with different numbers of neutrons. The number of protons plus neutrons in an atom is the mass number.

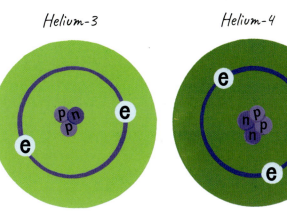

Helium-3

Helium-4

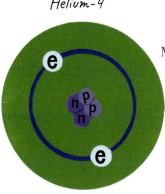

Most helium atoms are isotope helium-4, which has two neutrons (4 is its mass number). Helium-3 has only one neutron (3 is its mass number).

21

Elements

There are millions of chemicals, but just 118 are elements. Elements are the simplest chemicals. They can't be broken down into any other substance. All other chemicals are elements combined.

Around 90 elements occur naturally. The others are synthetic—human-made. Every element has atoms that are all the same and different to atoms of other elements.

WHAT IS AN ATOM?: PAGE 20

All the elements are listed in the Periodic Table. You know some of them well.

Some are less familiar.

Iridium is a metal. It makes colorful compounds, and it's named after Iris, goddess of rainbows.

Selenium is a nonmetal used in dandruff shampoo. Its name means "moon."

Einsteinium is a synthetic, radioactive metal, named after Einstein.

Elements can be metals, nonmetals, or semimetals. They all have their own properties. Some are radioactive.

We use carbon as graphite in pencils.

1 H Hydrogen

Hydrogen has the symbol H and atomic number 1.

Names, numbers, and symbols

Every element has a name and a chemical symbol made of one or two letters. Phosphorus is P. Silver is Ag. Every element has an atomic number.

THE PERIODIC TABLE: PAGES 36–37

PROTONS: PAGE 21

MORE

All matter contains atoms of at least one element. Pure elements are sometimes found in nature. A nugget of gold is a pure element. All its atoms are gold atoms.

PURE AND IMPURE: PAGE 12

Elements can mix without combining chemically, such as in air.

Elements combine chemically when their atoms bond to make molecules. These are new chemicals—they are compounds.

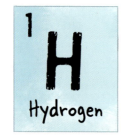

One carbon and two oxygen atoms combine to make carbon dioxide.

The process of elements combining to form different chemicals is a reaction.

MIXTURES: PAGE 12

MOLECULES: PAGE 26

COMPOUNDS: PAGE 24

REACTIONS: PAGE 30

Metals

Metals are generally solid, strong, and shiny. They are good conductors of electricity.

Molybdenum has a very high melting point. It's used to make temperature-resistant alloys.

Molybdenum

Molybdenum–steel alloy was used to build the Louvre pyramid in Paris.

ALLOYS: PAGE 43

Nonmetals

Nonmetals are often light and brittle. They don't conduct electricity.

Sulfur is a crystalline nonmetal. It makes smelly compounds—some of them are found in skunk spray.

Sulfur   Skunk

CRYSTAL LATTICES: PAGE 27

Semimetals

Seven elements are semimetals. They sometimes conduct electricity.

Silicon

Pure silicon looks like a metal, but doesn't conduct like one.

SEMIMETALS: PAGE 44

Radioactive

Radioactive elements are unstable—their atoms decay (break up). Synthetic elements and some natural isotopes are radioactive.

Radioactive americium is used in smoke detectors.

THE HEAVIEST ELEMENTS: PAGE 46

ISOTOPES: PAGE 21

States of matter

At room temperature, most elements are solid, eleven are gases, and two—mercury and bromine—are liquids.

Bromine is a dark red non-metal liquid.

Mercury is a silver liquid metal.

A trick spoon made of gallium melts in warm water. Its melting point is 30 °C (86 °F).

CHANGING STATES: PAGE 11

Compounds

When elements react and combine, they make new chemicals with different properties. The possible combinations of fewer than 100 elements produce millions of compounds that make up our world and the rest of the Universe.

A compound:
- has molecules containing atoms of more than one element.
- can only be separated into elements by a chemical reaction.
- contains a definite ratio of elements.
- contains bonded—chemically joined—elements.
- has different properties to the elements it contains.

Carbonated water is a mixture of two compounds—water and carbon dioxide.

Water is a compound of two gases—hydrogen and oxgyen in the ratio 2:1.

Carbon dioxide is a compound of an element we often see as a solid (carbon) and a gas (oxygen) in the ratio 1:2.

ELEMENTS: PAGE 22

BONDING: PAGE 28

MOLECULES: PAGE 26

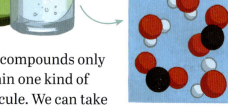

Pure compounds only contain one kind of molecule. We can take the carbon dioxide out of carbonated water, leaving pure water.

We can't take the elements out of the molecules without chemically changing the compounds.

Pure and impure chemicals have different properties. Adding salt (an impurity) changes the boiling point and freezing point of water.

PURE AND IMPURE: PAGE 12

When elements combine, the name of the new compound comes from the elements' names. Naming of simple compounds follows three rules:

Rule 1

The name of a compound of two elements generally ends in -ide. Magnesium chloride ($MgCl_2$) and boron carbide (B_4C) are examples.

Magnesium chloride is a food supplement.

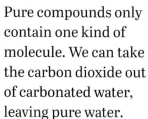

Boron carbide—used in military vehicles and bulletproof vests—is a boron-carbon compound.

Rule 2

In the name of a compound of two elements, the name of the element to the left in the Periodic Table comes first. Find carbon and oxygen to see why carbon dioxide (CO_2) isn't called dioxygen carbide.

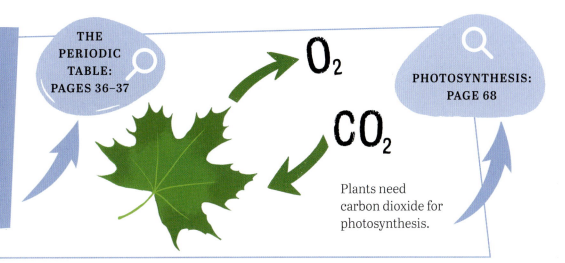

THE PERIODIC TABLE: PAGES 36–37

PHOTOSYNTHESIS: PAGE 68

Plants need carbon dioxide for photosynthesis.

Rule 3

The name of a compound of three elements, including oxygen, ends in -ate or -ite.

Calcium carbonate ($CaCO_3$), or limestone, is a compound of calcium, carbon, and oxygen.

Sodium chlorite ($NaClO_2$) is a compound of sodium, chlorine, and oxygen.

Calcium carbonate makes beautiful natural limestone pools in Pamukkale, Turkey.

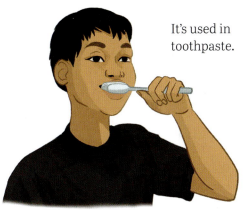

It's used in toothpaste.

Compounds can have several names. Their chemical formulae avoid confusion.

Methane (CH_4) is also known as methyl hydride, marsh gas, or natural gas.

METHANE: PAGE 71

FORMULAE: PAGE 26

NanoKid's chemical formula is $C_{39}H_{42}O_2$.

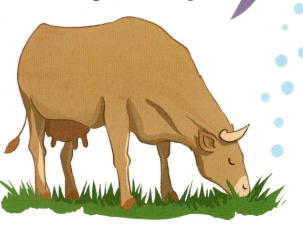

Grazing animals expel methane from both ends!

Organic compounds can have very long names.

NanoKid is an organic compound that scientists created in a fun shape. Its standard name is 2-[4-[2-[3,5-bis(pent-1-ynyl)phenyl]ethynyl]-2,5-bis(3,3-dimethylbut-1-ynyl)phenyl]-1,3-dioxolane.

Molecules and molecular structures

Molecules with different kinds of atoms are the smallest particles of compounds. When atoms join up into molecules, they create the building blocks of all other chemicals.

Molecules are bonded groups of atoms. Typical molecules have a countable number of atoms—a water molecule has three atoms. Other molecular structures—such as sodium chloride—are lattices with variable numbers of atoms or ions.

ELEMENTS: PAGE 22

DIATOMIC ELEMENTS: PAGE 28

COMPOUNDS: PAGE 24

If a molecule has atoms all the same, it is an element.

Hydrogen (H_2) is a diatomic element.

If there are at least two different atoms in a molecule, then it is a compound.

A methane molecule has one carbon and four hydrogen atoms. Its chemical formula is CH_4.

Chemical formulae

A chemical formula is a short, clear way to identify a chemical. It uses numbers and chemical symbols. It shows either the number of atoms in a molecule, or the ratio of atoms or ions in a molecular structure.

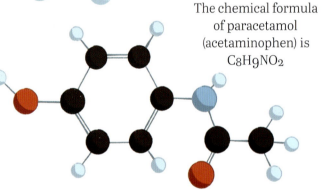

The chemical formula of paracetamol (acetaminophen) is $C_8H_9NO_2$

A paracetamol (acetaminophen) molecule has eight carbon, nine hydrogen, one nitrogen, and two oxygen atoms.

Some examples of molecules and molecular structures are:

- Lattices
- Allotropes
- Organic molecules

Structural formulae

Structural formulae show how atoms are bonded together.

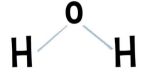

The structural formula of a water molecule (H_2O) shows that the atoms are arranged at an angle.

Ball-and-stick diagrams and models use simple colored balls as atoms. Here are more structural images of a water molecule:

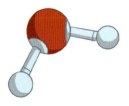

Lattices

The atoms or ions in a lattice form a regular, repeating, three-dimensional, crystal structure that can be small or large.

Ionic Lattices

Metal compounds make a giant lattice with ionic bonds. Sodium chloride—table salt—has formula NaCl because the ratio of sodium to chlorine ions is 1:1.

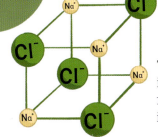

Salt crystals seen under a magnifying lens have straight edges and right angles because of the ionic lattice.

This diagram shows eight ions—but there can be 1,200,000,000,000,000,000 ions in one salt crystal.

Covalent Lattices

Some nonmetals form a giant lattice, with covalent bonds.

COVALENT BONDS: PAGE 29

Silicon dioxide—sand—has formula SiO_2 because the ratio of silicon to oxygen atoms is 1:2.

● Silicon
● Oxygen

The molecules in a sandcastle are as amazing as the castle.

Diamond is another giant covalent structure.

Allotropes

Diamond and graphite are allotropes—different forms—of carbon. The atoms bond in different patterns.

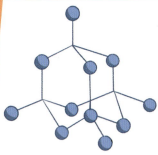

Diamond is hard because its structure is strong in all directions.

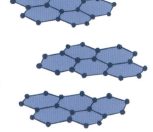

Graphite is soft because the atoms form sheets that slide over each other.

Diamond is the hardest natural material and one of the most valuable.

Organic molecules

Organic molecules have carbon–hydrogen bonds. The carbon atoms form a chain, with atoms of hydrogen and a few other elements attached.

Hydrocarbons are organic molecules with just carbon and hydrogen atoms.

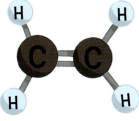

Ethylene (C_2H_4) is "unsaturated"—it contains a double bond.

Polymers are organic molecules.

Organic molecules found on Mars by NASA's *Perseverance* rover could suggest that the planet once had microscopic life.

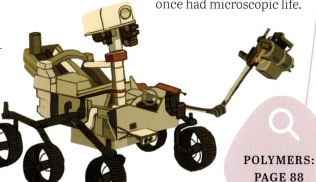

ORGANIC CHEMISTRY: PAGE 56

DOUBLE BONDS: PAGE 28

POLYMERS: PAGE 88

Bonding

Tiny atoms are able to build materials because they can make bonds. By joining together in all their combinations, atoms create molecules of all the compounds in the Universe.

Chemical bonds are created by electrons in the atoms' outer electron shells. The bonds are made when electrons are shared, gained, or lost during chemical reactions.

REACTIONS: PAGE 30

WHAT IS AN ATOM?: PAGE 20

Some types of bonds are:
- Covalent
- Ionic
- Metallic

The first electron shell of an atom can hold two electrons. The second shell can hold eight. Full shells are stable. Atoms with full outer shells are unreactive and don't make bonds.

Atoms with fewer electrons than they can hold are unstable. They react with other atoms to get a full outer shell.

Linus Pauling won the Nobel Prize for Chemistry in 1954 for research into atomic bonding. He later won the Nobel Peace Prize for campaigning against nuclear weapons.

NOBLE GASES: PAGE 41

A fluorine atom has seven electrons in its outer shell. It attracts an electron from another atom to gain a full shell.

A magnesium atom has two electrons in its outer shell. It gives them away, and the shell underneath—which is full—becomes the outer shell.

MORE

Single, double, and triple bonds

Some atoms share two or three electrons with one other atom. This makes a double or triple covalent bond.

Some diatomic (2-atom) elements show this kind of bonding.

Two pairs of electrons make a double bond in oxygen (O_2).

Three pairs of electrons make a triple bond in nitrogen (N_2).

Hydrogen (H_2) has a single bond.

Hydrogen

Oxygen

Nitrogen

A double bond is a much stronger connection than a single bond.

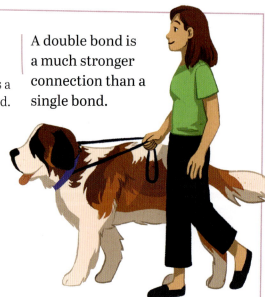

NITROGEN CYCLE: PAGE 72

28

Covalent bonds

Two atoms sharing a pair of electrons makes one covalent bond.

A dot-and-cross diagram of a water (H_2O) molecule shows its two covalent bonds. The two hydrogen atoms each gain one electron, and the oxygen atom gains two electrons.

Hydrocarbons supply heat because when they burn, their covalent bonds release a lot of energy as they break.

STRUCTURAL FORMULAE: PAGE 26

COMBUSTION: PAGE 31

Ionic bonds

Metal atoms react with nonmetals by donating (giving) electrons. Atoms that lose or gain an electron become ions (charged particles).

Ions that have lost an electron have a positive charge. Ions that gained an electron have a negative charge. The opposite charges attract, forming an ionic bond.

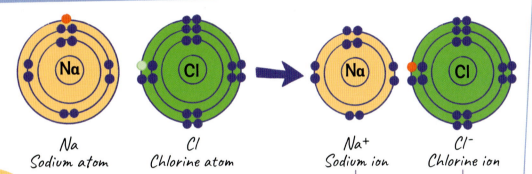

Na
Sodium atom

Cl
Chlorine atom

Na^+
Sodium ion

Cl^-
Chlorine ion

Sodium Chloride (NaCl)

A sodium atom donates an electron to a chlorine atom to make sodium chloride (NaCl).

I think I lost an electron!

Are you positive?

The repeating pattern forms a giant ionic structure.

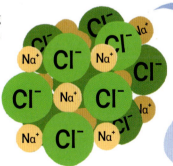

IONIC LATTICES: PAGE 27

Metallic bonds

Metals are structures of positively charged ions. The outer shell electrons are free to move about. Attraction between the ions and the electrons makes metallic bonds. The electrons carry an electric charge, so metals conduct electricity.

Metallic bonding in sodium

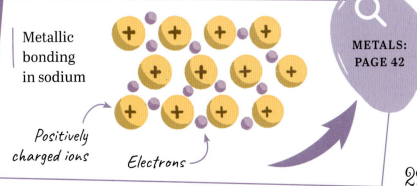

Positively charged ions

Electrons

METALS: PAGE 42

29

Reactions

Chemicals are transformed in chemical reactions. Their atoms swap places and rearrange into new groups that are different chemicals with new properties.

The chemicals at the start of a reaction are the reactants. The chemicals at the end are the products.

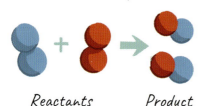

Reactants   *Product*

Reactions can involve atoms, molecules, or ions. The particles form new products by moving around, colliding, breaking bonds, rearranging, and bonding in different groups.

- Mass is conserved—no atoms are lost or made. The product weighs the same as the reactants.
- The original reactants can't be restored.

BONDING: PAGE 28

COMPOUNDS: PAGE 24

ELEMENT SYMBOLS: PAGE 22

CHEMICAL FORMULAE: PAGE 26

Equations

Equations describe reactions.

In a combination (or synthesis) reaction, two elements combine to make one compound.

Iron   *Sulfur*

Iron Sulfide

Iron and sulfur combine to form iron sulfide.

The word equation for the reaction is:

Iron + sulfur → iron sulfide

The chemical equation uses symbols and formulae:

$Fe + S \rightarrow FeS$

It shows ratios—one atom of iron reacts with one atom of sulfur to produce one molecule of iron sulfide.

Other types of reaction are:
- Oxidation
- Hydrogenation
- Thermal decomposition
- Neutralization
- Displacement

MORE

Evidence

Evidence of a reaction could be:
- A temperature change
- A color change
- Gas bubbles
- Smelly fumes
- An explosion

REACTION RATES: PAGE 32

Oxidation

A substance gaining oxygen atoms. Sliced apple and banana skin turn brown when compounds react with oxygen.

Combustion (burning) is an oxidation reaction.

When hydrocarbon fuels, such as wax or methane (CH_4) burn, they react with oxygen to produce carbon dioxide and water.

methane + oxygen → carbon dioxide + water

$$CH_4 + 2O_2 \rightarrow CO_2 + 2H_2O$$

Heat and light energy is also produced.

HYDRO-CARBONS: PAGE 27

ENERGY: PAGE 32

Corrosion is oxidation. Metals react with oxygen to form metal oxides. **Rusting** is iron corroding to form iron oxide (rust).

Burning and rusting are irreversible—we can't get the reactants back.

Hydrogenation

Hydrogenation is when a compound gains hydrogen atoms. When hydrogen is added to unsaturated hydrocarbons, the double bonds become single.

Hydrogenation of vegetable oils makes margarine.

ORGANIC MOLECULES: PAGE 27

Thermal decomposition

Heating breaks down one compound into simpler chemicals.

Carbon dioxide produced from the breakdown of sodium bicarbonate (baking soda) makes a baking cake rise.

ELECTROLYSIS: PAGE 58

Electrolysis is another form of decomposition.

Displacement

More reactive elements displace—push out—less reactive elements from compounds.

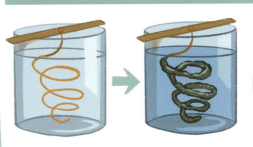

REACTIVITY SERIES: PAGE 43

Neutralization

Acids and alkalis neutralize each other to produce a salt and water.

sodium hydroxide + hydrochloric acid → sodium chloride + water

$$NaOH + HCl \rightarrow NaCl + H2O$$

Sodium chloride is table salt.

ACIDS AND ALKALIS: PAGE 16

Copper wire displaces silver from silver nitrate solution and forms blue copper nitrate. The silver forms crystals on the wire.

Reaction rates and energy

Reactions involve a transfer of energy, and the particles need enough energy to start with. We can change the conditions to control a reaction and the speed it happens.

If colliding particles don't have enough energy to react, they just bounce off each other. The amount of energy that they need is their **activation energy**.

The **rate of reaction** is the time taken for all reactants to become products.

Gasoline (petrol) fumes and oxygen mix harmlessly until a spark provides the energy they need to explode.

REACTIONS: PAGE 30

Reactions can be sped up by temperature, pressure, concentration, surface area, and catalysts.

MORE

Chemical energy

Chemical energy is stored inside the bonds that join atoms together in molecules.

The molecular bonds of fossil fuels, batteries, explosives, and food all store energy that we can use.

BONDING: PAGE 28

The Law of Conservation of Energy

Energy is never created or destroyed—it only changes from one form to another. Chemical energy can be transformed into other forms of energy, such as heat or electricity.

Car engines convert chemical energy in fuels to energy that moves the car.

BODY BIOCHEMISTRY: PAGE 76

Our bodies transform chemical energy from food into the energy we need to live.

Endothermic and exothermic

In chemical reactions, energy is absorbed when bonds break, and released when bonds are made. Overall, the reaction is either endothermic (absorbs energy) or exothermic (releases energy).

Many oxidation reactions are **exothermic**.

OXIDATION: PAGE 31

Composting is exothermic. Australian brush turkeys build a compost heap, and the decaying vegetable matter warms their eggs.

Photosynthesis is an **endothermic** reaction.

PHOTOSYNTHESIS: PAGE 68

Temperature

Heated particles move faster and collide more often with more energy, so more collisions result in a reaction.

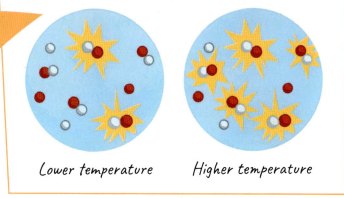

Lower temperature   Higher temperature

Pressure

Increasing pressure on a gas squashes the particles into a smaller space, and they collide and react more often.

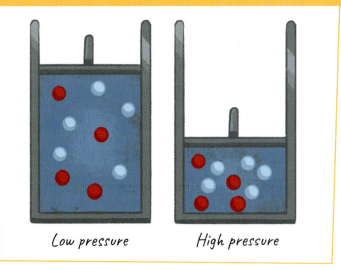

Low pressure   High pressure

Concentration

Increasing concentration of a gas or liquid in a solution makes the particles more crowded, leading to more collisions.

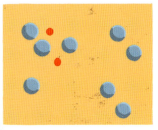 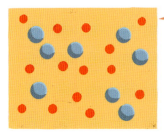

Lower concentration   Higher concentration

SOLUTIONS:
PAGE 12

Surface area

Increasing surface area makes more room for collisions. Small pieces react faster than a big lump.

Smaller surface area   Larger surface area

Catalysts

Catalysts lower the activation energy particles need to react, so more collisions result in a reaction.

Catalysts* don't change and aren't used up, so they can be reused.

Some catalysts give particles a place to bond before they move on as products.

Catalyst   Reactants bonding   Release of product

*Enzymes are biological catalysts.

ENZYMES:
PAGE 74

33

Organizing elements

The Periodic Table is a system of organizing the elements by the size of their atoms, from smallest to biggest. We can predict a lot about an element from its place on the Table.

THE PERIODIC TABLE: PAGE 36

ELEMENTS: PAGE 22

We read the Periodic Table from the top left, along the rows and down the columns, to the bottom-right corner. There are 118 squares—one for each element. There are 18 vertical columns—the Groups. There are seven rows—the Periods.

Atomic number

You can find any element on the Table from its atomic number—the number of protons in one atom.

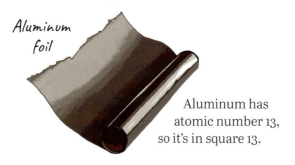

Aluminum foil

Aluminum has atomic number 13, so it's in square 13.

Periodicity

The Table shows a repeated pattern—periodicity—which lets us predict elements' properties. For example, Periods always start with a reactive metal in Group 1, and end with an unreactive nonmetal in Group 18.

The periodicity is due to atomic structure. Each new electron shell begins a new Period. Atoms in Period 1 have one shell, atoms in Period 2 have two shells, and so on.

Lithium and neon are both in Period 2.

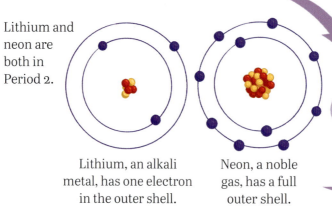

Lithium, an alkali metal, has one electron in the outer shell.

Neon, a noble gas, has a full outer shell.

The Table groups metals, nonmetals, semimetals, lanthanides, and actinides near each other.

PREDICTIONS: PAGE 48

ATOMIC STRUCTURE: PAGE 20

The elements in a vertical Group all have the same number of electrons in their outer shells, so their reactivity and other properties are similar. Atoms down the Group have more shells, so the Group's properties show trends.

ALKALI METALS: PAGE 41

NOBLE GASES: PAGE 41

REACTIONS: PAGE 30

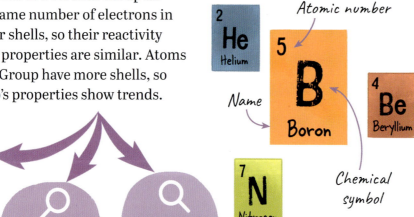

2 He Helium

Atomic number

5 B Boron

Name

4 Be Beryllium

7 N Nitrogen

Chemical symbol

The squares

Each square shows the chemical symbol and atomic number for one element. It also tells us more—such as, one boron atom has five protons and five electrons, it's in Period 2, and it has two electrons in its first shell and three electrons in its second shell.

Metals

Most elements are metals on the left and center of the Table.

Gold

Iron and gold are typical metals.

Iron

METALS: PAGE 42

Nonmetals

The nonmetals are to the right.

Nonmetals build living things.

NONMETALS: PAGE 45

Semimetals

Seven semimetals (metalloids) zigzag in a line between metals and nonmetals.

SEMIMETALS: PAGE 44

Electronic devices rely on semimetals.

Lanthanides and actinides

These 30 metals are in extra rows that "pop out" of the Table.

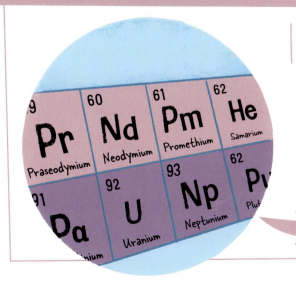

Lanthanides are atomic numbers 57 to 71. Actinides are 89 to 103.

LANTHANIDES AND ACTINIDES: PAGE 43

The history

The Periodic Table is based on Dmitri Mendeleev's system from 1869. Mendeleev predicted the properties of elements that were discovered later.

Dmitri Mendeleev

The Periodic Table

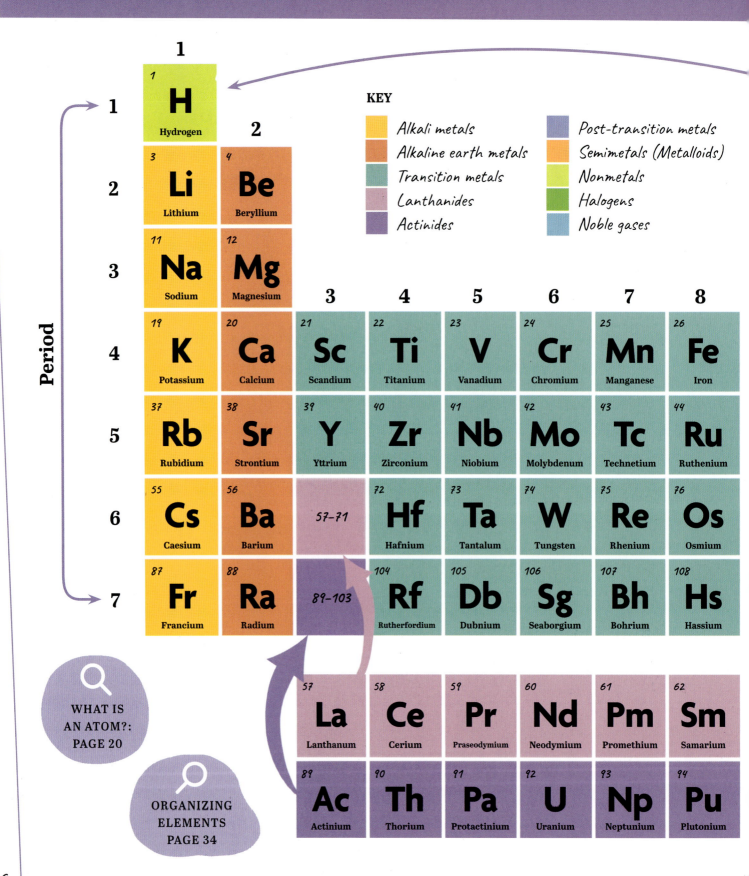

KEY

- Alkali metals
- Alkaline earth metals
- Transition metals
- Lanthanides
- Actinides
- Post-transition metals
- Semimetals (Metalloids)
- Nonmetals
- Halogens
- Noble gases

Period

1

1	2		3	4	5	6	7	8
1 **H** Hydrogen								
3 **Li** Lithium	**4** **Be** Beryllium							
11 **Na** Sodium	**12** **Mg** Magnesium							
19 **K** Potassium	**20** **Ca** Calcium		**21** **Sc** Scandium	**22** **Ti** Titanium	**23** **V** Vanadium	**24** **Cr** Chromium	**25** **Mn** Manganese	**26** **Fe** Iron
37 **Rb** Rubidium	**38** **Sr** Strontium		**39** **Y** Yttrium	**40** **Zr** Zirconium	**41** **Nb** Niobium	**42** **Mo** Molybdenum	**43** **Tc** Technetium	**44** **Ru** Ruthenium
55 **Cs** Caesium	**56** **Ba** Barium	57–71	**72** **Hf** Hafnium	**73** **Ta** Tantalum	**74** **W** Tungsten	**75** **Re** Rhenium	**76** **Os** Osmium
87 **Fr** Francium	**88** **Ra** Radium	89–103	**104** **Rf** Rutherfordium	**105** **Db** Dubnium	**106** **Sg** Seaborgium	**107** **Bh** Bohrium	**108** **Hs** Hassium

57	58	59	60	61	62
La Lanthanum	**Ce** Cerium	**Pr** Praseodymium	**Nd** Neodymium	**Pm** Promethium	**Sm** Samarium
89 **Ac** Actinium	90 **Th** Thorium	91 **Pa** Protactinium	92 **U** Uranium	93 **Np** Neptunium	94 **Pu** Plutonium

WHAT IS
AN ATOM?:
PAGE 20

ORGANIZING
ELEMENTS
PAGE 34

The Periodic Table displays the 118 elements. Elements are substances that are made of only one type of atom and cannot be broken down into simpler substances. Alone or with each other, the elements form all the materials we can see and touch.

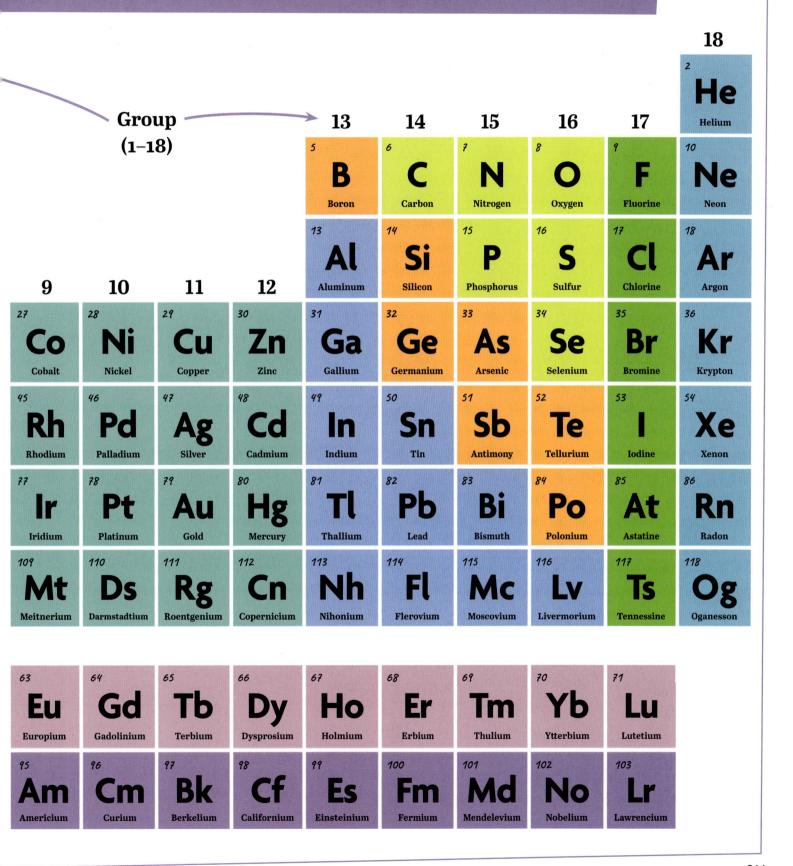

Group (1–18)

18
2 **He** Helium

13	14	15	16	17	
5 **B** Boron	6 **C** Carbon	7 **N** Nitrogen	8 **O** Oxygen	9 **F** Fluorine	10 **Ne** Neon
13 **Al** Aluminum	14 **Si** Silicon	15 **P** Phosphorus	16 **S** Sulfur	17 **Cl** Chlorine	18 **Ar** Argon

9	10	11	12
27 **Co** Cobalt	28 **Ni** Nickel	29 **Cu** Copper	30 **Zn** Zinc
45 **Rh** Rhodium	46 **Pd** Palladium	47 **Ag** Silver	48 **Cd** Cadmium
77 **Ir** Iridium	78 **Pt** Platinum	79 **Au** Gold	80 **Hg** Mercury
109 **Mt** Meitnerium	110 **Ds** Darmstadtium	111 **Rg** Roentgenium	112 **Cn** Copernicium

31 **Ga** Gallium	32 **Ge** Germanium	33 **As** Arsenic	34 **Se** Selenium	35 **Br** Bromine	36 **Kr** Krypton
49 **In** Indium	50 **Sn** Tin	51 **Sb** Antimony	52 **Te** Tellurium	53 **I** Iodine	54 **Xe** Xenon
81 **Tl** Thallium	82 **Pb** Lead	83 **Bi** Bismuth	84 **Po** Polonium	85 **At** Astatine	86 **Rn** Radon
113 **Nh** Nihonium	114 **Fl** Flerovium	115 **Mc** Moscovium	116 **Lv** Livermorium	117 **Ts** Tennessine	118 **Og** Oganesson

63 **Eu** Europium	64 **Gd** Gadolinium	65 **Tb** Terbium	66 **Dy** Dysprosium	67 **Ho** Holmium	68 **Er** Erbium	69 **Tm** Thulium	70 **Yb** Ytterbium	71 **Lu** Lutetium
95 **Am** Americium	96 **Cm** Curium	97 **Bk** Berkelium	98 **Cf** Californium	99 **Es** Einsteinium	100 **Fm** Fermium	101 **Md** Mendelevium	102 **No** Nobelium	103 **Lr** Lawrencium

The lightest elements

The elements with the smallest atoms are hydrogen and helium. They are both low-density, invisible gases with no smell—but they are not alike in other ways.

Hydrogen and helium are the only elements in Period 1 of the Periodic Table. They're so light, they escape into space from our atmosphere.

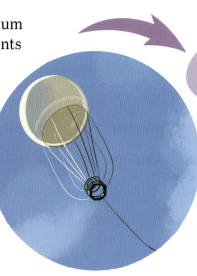

THE PERIODIC TABLE: PAGES 36–37

Hydrogen and helium are both used in weather balloons.

Hydrogen and helium are very different in reactivity, commercial production, and uses.

The Atoms

Hydrogen has one proton and one electron. Ninety-nine percent of hydrogen atoms are protium, which has no neutrons, but hydrogen also has two more isotopes. Deuterium has one neutron, and tritium has two.

Helium has two protons plus two neutrons. It is produced when hydrogen nuclei fuse, inside stars. The fusion also produces energy.

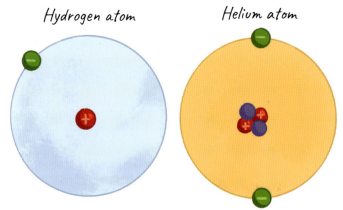

Hydrogen atom

Helium atom

- Electron
+ Proton
- Neutron

Deuterium

Tritium

Nuclear fusion to produce helium

Helium

Energy

Neutron

The Sun's heat and light are from hydrogen fusion.

ISOTOPES: PAGE 21

Abundance

Hydrogen and helium were the first atoms to form, and they are the most abundant. A quarter of all atoms in the Universe are helium—almost three-quarters are hydrogen.

On Earth, hydrogen (H_2) makes up only about 0.5 ppm (parts per million) of the atmosphere, and helium makes up about 5.2 ppm. More hydrogen is found in the crust, but helium is found only in tiny amounts.

THE UNIVERSE: PAGE 62

Reactivity

Hydrogen

Hydrogen is very reactive and explodes with oxygen. Hydrogen atoms bond with each other or in compounds. It forms organic chemicals with carbon, and it's essential for life.

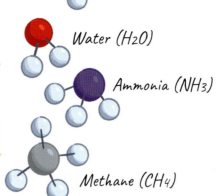

Diatomic hydrogen (H_2)

Water (H_2O)

Ammonia (NH_3)

Methane (CH_4)

ORGANIC MOLECULES: PAGE 27

COVALENT BONDS: PAGE 29

Helium

Helium is unreactive and nonflammable. It doesn't bond, and it's not important for life.

Helium (He)

Production

Hydrogen

Hydrogen is produced from natural gas and by electrolysis.

Electricity breaks down water into hydrogen and oxygen.

ELECTRO-CHEMISTRY: PAGE 58

Helium

Small amounts of helium are made by radioactive decay of uranium. It's extracted from natural gas, but it can't be manufactured.

THE HEAVIEST ELEMENTS: PAGE 46

One day, we might have fusion that produces helium and clean energy, like the Sun.

Uses

Hydrogen

Hydrogen is used to make chemicals, fertilizers, plastics, and medicines.

It makes electricity to run electric cars.

It's a fuel for rocket engines.

CARS: PAGE 91

Helium

Helium cools the giant magnets in hospital MRI scanners and the Large Hadron Collider.

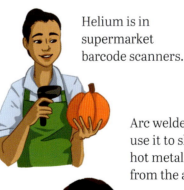

Helium is in supermarket barcode scanners.

Arc welders use it to shield hot metals from the air.

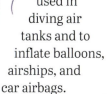

SEEING ATOMS AND MOLECULES: PAGE 60

It's also used in diving air tanks and to inflate balloons, airships, and car airbags.

Element groups

Vertical Groups of the Periodic Table are like families. Their elements have shared characteristics that show trends. We can predict how an element will look and behave by its position in the Group.

Trends in properties are clearly seen in elements on the right and left of the Table (Groups 1–2 and 13–18*).

THE PERIODIC TABLE: PAGES 36–37

REACTIONS: PAGE 30

Some Groups that show trends are:

- Alkali metal
- Alkaline earth metals
- Halogens
- Noble gases

Reactivity trends

Elements in a Group show trends because electrons closer to the nucleus are held more tightly or attracted more strongly.

Lithium

Sodium

Potassium

The very reactive elements in Group 1 bond by readily giving away one electron.

Lithium is the least reactive because its nucleus holds the electron more tightly than its bigger relatives do.

Fluorine

Chlorine

Bromine

Group 17 elements bond by attracting an electron from another atom.

Fluorine is the most reactive because its nucleus attracts other electrons more strongly than its bigger relatives.

IONIC BONDS: PAGE 29

PREDICTIONS: PAGE 48

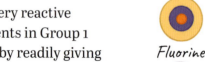
Increasing reactivity

ATOMIC STRUCTURE: PAGE 20

Increasing reactivity

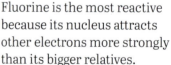
They say opposites attract!

And they're right.

NaCl

Sodium chloride is a good example of Group 1 and Group 17 getting together!

Physical trends

Melting points are a physical property. The low melting points of Group 1 metals show a trend.

Lithium is soft and melts at 180 °C (356 °F), potassium is softer and melts at 63 °C (145 °F), and caesium is very soft and melts in a warm room at 28 °C (82 °F).

Group 1 metals are soft enough to cut.

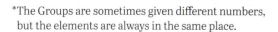

*The Groups are sometimes given different numbers, but the elements are always in the same place.

Group 1—Alkali metals

Alkali metals are silvery and shiny, but quickly go dull (tarnish).

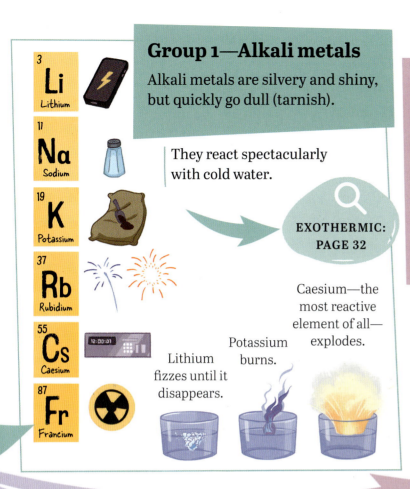

They react spectacularly with cold water.

EXOTHERMIC: PAGE 32

Caesium—the most reactive element of all—explodes.

Lithium fizzes until it disappears.

Potassium burns.

Group 2—Alkaline earth metals

Alkaline earth metals are almost as reactive as Group 1 elements. Magnesium fizzes in water, and the reaction gets faster through calcium, strontium, and barium.

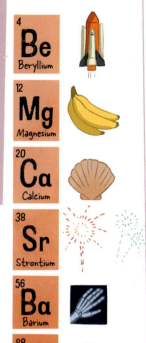

Beryllium and magnesium are very light. Barium is much heavier and absorbs X-rays in medical tests.

METALS: PAGE 42

Group 17—Halogens

The halogens are nonmetals. Fluorine and chlorine are greenish gases, bromine is a dark red liquid, and iodine is a purple-black solid.

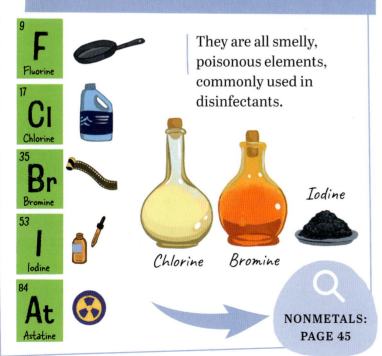

They are all smelly, poisonous elements, commonly used in disinfectants.

Chlorine

Bromine

Iodine

NONMETALS: PAGE 45

Group 18—Noble gases

The noble gases are unreactive because their atoms' shells are full of electrons. They have low boiling points that get higher going down the group.

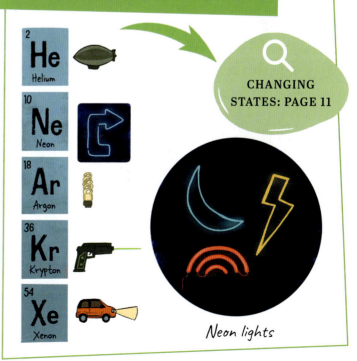

CHANGING STATES: PAGE 11

Neon lights

Metals

Most metals, but not all, are strong, hard materials with properties that make them valuable for building bridges, making musical instruments, or carrying electricity.

THE PERIODIC TABLE: PAGES 36–37

Around 80% of elements are metals. The transition metals, in the central block of the Periodic Table, are "typical" metals.

Transition metals usually have these properties:

- High melting and boiling points
- Good conductors of heat and electricity
- High density—solid and heavy
- Shiny
- Strong
- Malleable—can be shaped
- Ductile—can be pulled into wires
- Sonorous

Bell metal (bronze) gives gongs a sonorous "ring."

Copper is good for electrical wiring.

Precious metals are used in coins and jewelry.

WE BUY GOLD SILVER

OPEN

Besides transition metals, other metal groups include:

- alkali metals
- alkaline earth metals
- lanthanides
- actinides
- post-transition metals.

Iron filings show the magnetic field around a bar magnet.

N   S

Iron, nickel, and cobalt are magnetic. They can be made into magnets.

MATERIALS AND PROPERTIES: PAGE 14

Alkali metals

Group 1 metals are very reactive and low-density.

Caesium is the only golden metal element besides gold and copper.

Alkaline earth metals

Group 2 metals are soft, reactive metals.

Magnesium burns easily with a bright-white light.

Their compounds give color to fireworks.

GROUP 1: PAGE 41

GROUP 2: PAGE 41

Lanthanides

Element numbers 57–71 are soft, reactive metals, often found combined in ores.

Lanthanum and cerium are used in misch metal alloy for fire sticks and lighters.

Actinides

Element numbers 89–103 are all radioactive.

THE HEAVIEST ELEMENTS: PAGE 46

Depleted (low-radioactivity) uranium is used as ballast and weights for ships and aircraft.

Post-transition metals

Metals in Groups 13 to 16 are weaker and have lower melting and boiling points than the transition metals. They are also called "basic" or "poor" metals.

Aluminum is in drinks cans, window frames, and aircraft.

Steel is lined with tin to make food "tins," or cans.

Alloys

Bronze (tin and copper) was the first alloy (mixture of metals).

Steel (iron and carbon) is stronger and lighter than iron and doesn't rust as easily. Added chromium makes stainless steel.

Steel is used in tools, vehicles, and buildings.

BRONZE AGE: PAGE 18

RUSTING: PAGE 31

Reactions of Metals

Metals bond by giving away electrons.

Metals react with acids to make a salt plus hydrogen.

When metals react with oxygen, they form basic oxides that make alkaline solutions with water.

Transition metals such as chromium make colorful compounds and solutions.

IONIC BONDS: PAGE 29

ACIDS AND ALKALIS: PAGE 16

Reactivity

The reactivity series lists metals by how readily they react. More reactive metals give more violent reactions.

Carbon (a non-metal) displaces less reactive metals. It's used to extract pure metals from their mineral ores.

Increasing activity

Potassium
Sodium
Lithium
Calcium
Magnesium
Aluminium
(Carbon)
Zinc
Iron
Copper
Silver
Gold

OUR WORLD: PAGE 64

DISPLACEMENT: PAGE 31

Nonmetals and Semimetals

There are fewer nonmetal elements than metals, and even fewer semimetals. Semimetals make our electronic devices work. The nonmetals, especially carbon, are essential for life.

The Periodic Table is divided by a line that zigzags from boron in Group 13 to polonium in Group 16. The elements to the left are metals. The elements to the right are nonmetals. The elements around the zigzag line have in-between properties. They are semi-metals, or metalloids.

THE PERIODIC TABLE: PAGES 36–37

Semimetals are boron, silicon, arsenic, germanium, antimony, tellurium, and polonium.

Semimetals

Semimetals sometimes have properties like metals, and sometimes like nonmetals.

Common properties of semimetals are:

- They are solids, and some allotropes look metallic.
- They sometimes conduct electricity.
- They are brittle, like nonmetals.
- They behave like metals in alloys.

ALLOTROPES: PAGE 27

Germanium

is used in optical fibers.

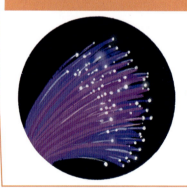

Boron

Baron makes superstrong magnets in alloys with neodymium and iron.

Silicon

Silicon doesn't conduct electricity, but adding **arsenic** makes "doped" silicon—which can conduct electricity.

A neodymium-iron-boron magnet holds many times its own weight.

Semiconductors make tiny electronics devices possible.

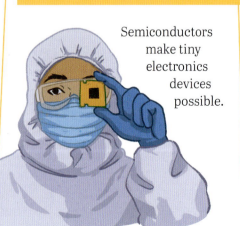

Antimony

Antimony is toxic but was used for centuries in medicines.

Ancient Egyptians used antimony eye makeup.

Tellurium

Tellurium makes metal alloys more workable. It's toxic and gives you "garlic breath!"

Pollonium

Pollonium is radioactive. It was used as a heat source for *Lunokhod* rovers exploring the Moon.

Nonmetals

The nonmetal elements are the noble gases and halogens, plus carbon, nitrogen, oxygen, phosphorus, sulfur, and selenium. Eleven nonmetals are gases at room temperature. One—bromine—is a liquid. The others are solids.

Nonmetals are generally:

- Insulators—poor conductors of heat and electricity
- Dull—they don't reflect light
- Low density—lightweight
- Brittle—they break easily and can't be shaped
- Weak
- Not magnetic
- Have low melting and boiling points

Nonmetals have "opposite" properties to metals.

Ceramics and plastics are nonmetal materials—they don't contain metals.

MATERIALS AND PROPERTIES: PAGE 14

HALOGENS: PAGE 41

NOBLE GASES: PAGE 41

Carbon makes diamond, pencil "lead"—and living things.

Sulfur is essential for life. Some bacteria—snottites—even use it for energy.

Nonmetal Reactions

Nonmetals bond with other nonmetals by sharing electrons. They bond with metals by taking electrons from the metal.

Nonmetals don't usually react with acids—but acids do attack nonmetals.

Nonmetals react with oxygen to form acidic oxides. Sulfur dioxide (SO_2), nitrogen oxides, and carbon dioxide are examples.

Sulfuric acid (H_2SO_4) is probably the most important industrial chemical. It's used in the oil and metals industries, and to manufacture fertilizers, explosives, dyes, adhesives, and wood preservatives.

In vulcanization, sulfur atoms form bridges linking long-chain rubber molecules. A tire of vulcanized rubber is one strong, giant molecule!

ACIDS AND ALKALIS: PAGE 16

BONDING: PAGE 29

REACTIONS: PAGE 30

SULFURIC ACID: PAGE 51

The heaviest elements

Most elements after lead (no. 82) on the Periodic Table are rare, and they are all radioactive. Radioactivity is very dangerous, but it also has important uses.

The atoms of the heaviest 36 elements are unstable. They fall apart—decay—by emitting particles or rays as radiation. The number of subatomic particles changes, so the element becomes a different isotope or element.

ISOTOPES: PAGE 21

ELEMENTS: PAGE 22

Radioactive nuclei don't all decay at once. An element's "half-life" is the time taken for half of its nuclei to decay.

Uranium-238 (with 92 protons and 146 neutrons) decays through 14 elements to become lead-206 (82 protons and 124 neutrons), which doesn't decay anymore.

Uranium's natural decay chain's first six steps are:

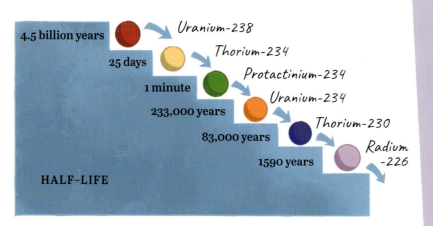

- 4.5 billion years — Uranium-238
- 25 days — Thorium-234
- 1 minute — Protactinium-234
- 233,000 years — Uranium-234
- 83,000 years — Thorium-230
- 1590 years — Radium-226

HALF-LIFE

Half a sample of uranium-238 takes 4.5 billion years to decay into thorium-234, but thorium-234's half-life is less than 25 days.

Uses of some of the heaviest elements are:

- Nuclear fission
- Safety
- Exploration
- Medicine
- War weapons
- Industry

Elements after uranium (no. 92) are hardly found in nature. They are made in nuclear reactors or by bashing other atoms and subatomic particles together, so they fuse into larger nuclei. Some synthetic elements' half-lives are less than a second.

THE PERIODIC TABLE: PAGES 36–37

MORE

Radioactive nuclei emit different types of radiation.

Paper blocks alpha particles; aluminum blocks beta particles; lead blocks gamma rays; concrete blocks neutrons.

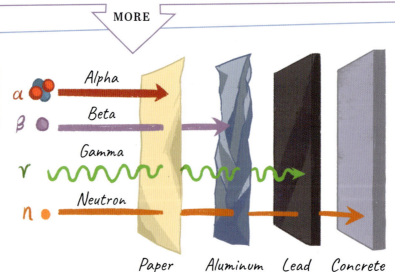

α Alpha

β Beta

γ Gamma

n Neutron

Paper   Aluminum   Lead   Concrete

The international radiation hazard sign.

46

Nuclear fission

Nuclear power plants bombard uranium with neutrons. The uranium nuclei split into smaller elements. The fission generates energy, used for electricity.

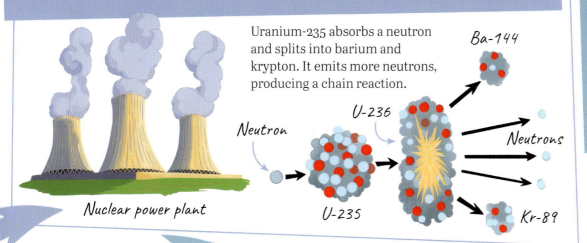

Nuclear power plant

Uranium-235 absorbs a neutron and splits into barium and krypton. It emits more neutrons, producing a chain reaction.

Neutron

U-236

U-235

Ba-144

Neutrons

Kr-89

Safety

Americium in a smoke alarm emits alpha particles that let an electric current flow. Smoke absorbs the particles and stops the current, setting off the alarm.

Exploration

Curium is used in space instruments that analyze rocks and soil.

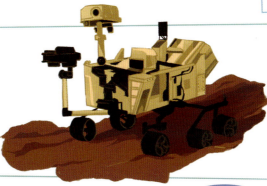

NASA's Mars *Curiosity* rover uses curium to investigate Mars' surface.

Medicine

Radium was first used to treat cancer in 1902 and is still sometimes used.

Doctors are testing astatine in new cancer treatments.

WORKING SCIENTIFICALLY: PAGE 48

War weapons

Uranium and plutonium were in deadly atom bombs used to end World War II.

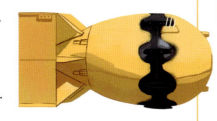

The "Fat Man" atom bomb devastated Nagasaki, Japan, in 1945.

Industry

Neutrons emitted by californium are used to measure oil and water layers in oil wells, find metal ores, and detect metal fatigue in aircraft.

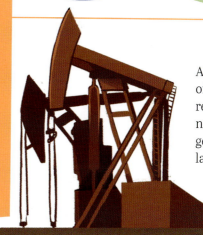

Absorption of neutrons reveals the nature of geological layers.

47

Working scientifically

Scientists ask questions and conduct investigations. They don't all work in a laboratory. An interest in science can lead to many different careers.

Like all scientists, chemists work scientifically. They think about something they've observed. They form a hypothesis—an idea to explain what they've seen. Then they predict what will happen in an experiment if one factor, such as temperature, is changed, and the hypothesis is correct. They test the prediction experimentally and draw conclusions from the results. This is scientific method.

In 1827, Robert Brown wondered why tiny pollen grains jiggle about in water. He hypothesized that it was because they were alive. He predicted that only fresh pollen would move— and he proved his hypothesis wrong by testing dried pollen. The dried grains still moved. It was an important negative result!

Water molecules make pollen grains move.

🔍 BROWNIAN MOTION: PAGE 11

School science can be the start of many careers. Here are a few ideas:

Working safely

Laboratories contain potential hazards, such as heat sources and explosive or corrosive chemicals. Understanding risks and working safely are essential to avoid getting hurt in any workplace.

MORE

Workers lower their risk of injury by following rules and taking safety precautions.

Warning signs you might see in a laboratory include:

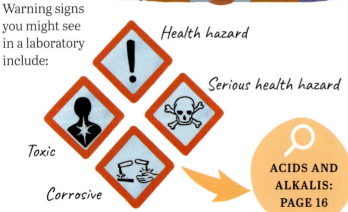

Health hazard

Serious health hazard

Toxic

Corrosive

🔍 ACIDS AND ALKALIS: PAGE 16

Chemical engineer

This engineer designs equipment and manufacturing processes to turn raw materials into chemicals and chemical-based products for industry.

🔍 INDUSTRIAL CHEMISTRY: PAGE 50

Environmental scientist

This scientist gathers information about pollutants in soil, water, or air, assessing risks and giving advice.

Forensic scientist

Forensic scientists investigate evidence from a crime scene, such as footprints, poisons, or DNA.

ANALYTICAL CHEMISTRY: PAGE 52

Laboratory technician

Giving practical support to research scientists, such as looking after laboratory equipment, a lab technician prepares and tests samples.

Materials chemist

A materials chemist develops new materials and finds materials with the right properties for new uses, often using computer modeling.

Argon is used in double glazing because it's a good heat insulator.

Glass panes

Argon gas

Seal

Pharmacist

A pharmacist prepares medicines and dispenses them to patients.

Pharmacologist

A pharmacologist develops safe medicines by studying how they work, often for pharmaceutical companies.

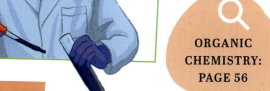

ORGANIC CHEMISTRY: PAGE 56

Sludge scientist

A sludge scientist turns sewage into useful products, such as methane for energy and solids for natural fertilizers.

Research scientist

A researcher works in a hospital gathering clinical data on treatments for diseases.

Industrial chemistry

Industrial chemistry involves all the reactions that transform raw materials into products. It manufactures large-scale chemicals and products to supply to commercial companies.

Industrial chemicals are made from raw materials (feedstocks). Some industrial chemicals may be feedstocks for making other chemicals, or they may be intermediates—reactants in the manufacturing steps for different products. Some are already finished products and have specialty uses, such as solvents or catalysts.

REACTIONS: PAGE 30

Three very large-scale industrial chemicals are: sulfuric acid, ethylene, and sodium hydroxide.

Chemicals are produced in factories or "plants."

Tanker trucks transport bulk chemicals by road.

Aldehydes are used in perfumes.

Crude oil is an important raw material for fuels, feedstocks, and chemicals called petrochemicals. It's processed (refined) by fractional distillation and cracking in an oil refinery.

Chemical engineers design processes to work efficiently. That means making as much product as possible, quickly, and at the lowest cost. Unwanted products or leftover reactants from a reaction are by-products. Finding uses for them reduces waste and lowers costs.

Glycerol is a by-product of manufacturing biodiesel fuel from agricultural crops. It can be turned into propanediol, which makes valuable chemicals including aldehydes.

FOSSIL FUELS: PAGE 90

MORE

Fractional distillation

Crude oil is a mixture of different-sized hydrocarbon molecules.

Crude oil is heated, and fractions are extracted as they evaporate and condense at different temperatures.

The different parts (fractions) are separated by fractional distillation.

ORGANIC CHEMISTRY: PAGE 56

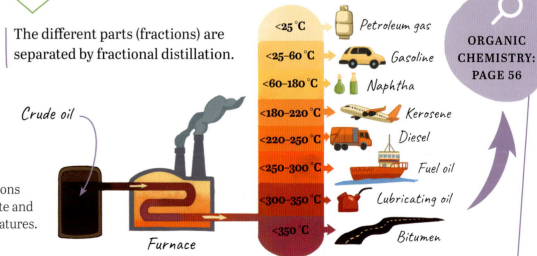

Crude oil

Furnace

<25 °C — Petroleum gas
<25–60 °C — Gasoline
<60–180 °C — Naphtha
<180–220 °C — Kerosene
<220–250 °C — Diesel
<250–300 °C — Fuel oil
<300–350 °C — Lubricating oil
<350 °C — Bitumen

Cracking

Some hydrocarbons from fractional distillation are broken down into smaller, more useful molecules. This is called "cracking"—a form of thermal decomposition. Zeolite catalysts lower the temperature for the reaction.

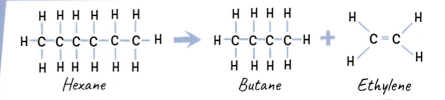

Cracking breaks a hexane molecule into butane and ethene.

THERMAL DECOMPOSITION: PAGE 31

Sulfuric acid

Around 320 million metric tons (292 million tons) of sulfuric acid (H_2SO_4) was produced worldwide in 2024. It makes fertilizers, detergents, explosives, dyes, fibers, pigments, and many other chemicals and medicines.

Ammonium sulfate fertilizer is made from sulfuric acid and ammonia.

It adds sulfur and nitrogen to soil.

AMMONIA: PAGE 55

Lead-acid car batteries contain sulfuric acid.

Ethylene

Ethylene, or ethene (C_2H_4), is a major organic feedstock. Global production is over 225 million metric tons (248 million tons) per year. Half of it goes to make polyethylene (polythene).

Ethylene is used to ripen fruit.

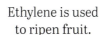

POLYMERS: PAGE 88

Ethylene glycol is an antifreeze used in cars and aircraft.

Sodium hydroxide

Sodium hydroxide, or caustic soda (NaOH), is produced with chlorine in the chlor-alkali process. Production is around 100 million metric tons (110 million tons) per year. It's a strong alkali, used in crude oil extraction, water treatment, and cleaning agents, and to make inorganic and organic chemicals.

Sodium hydroxide is used in papermaking and soap production.

Sodium hydroxide makes cocoa less bitter in chocolate.

CHLOR-ALKALI PROCESS: PAGE 59

Analytical chemistry

Analytical chemistry identifies the chemicals in substances. It can show the amount of compounds, where they came from, and even how they got there.

Chemicals are analyzed using controlled reactions and measurements. Careful sampling and testing skills are used in tasks ranging from identifying fibers at a crime scene, to checking for pollutants in a river, to studying ancient history.

Nickel in this 3,000-year-old iron arrow-head suggests the metal came from a meteorite that landed in Estonia around 1500 BCE.

Qualitative analysis identifies elements or compounds in a sample.

Quantitative analysis measures the amounts.

Products such as fertilizers and medicines are formulations—carefully designed mixtures of ingredients. Analysis during manufacturing makes sure that the formulation is correct and tests for impurities.

Quality control is essential in the production of medicines.

Simple laboratory analysis includes using reagents—compounds used to detect other chemicals—and testing properties, such as boiling points, which are changed by impurities.

Analytical methods include:

COMPOUNDS:
PAGE 24

Food tests

Reagents test for carbohydrates, proteins, and lipids (fats and oils) in food.

Yellowy-brown iodine turns potato blue-black, because starch is present.

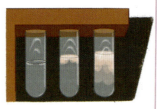

Proteins turn biuret's solution—copper sulfate and sodium hydroxide—from blue to purple.

Lipids go cloudy in alcohol and water.

Paper chromatography

In paper chromatography, water carries a sample up absorbent paper. Dissolved substances separate to form a chromatogram.

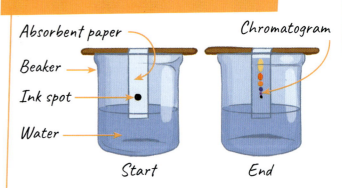

Absorbent paper
Chromatogram
Beaker
Ink spot
Water
Start
End

It works well with dyes, inks, and food colorants.

A form of chromatography is used to test for Covid-19.

Gas chromatography

Gas chromatography is quantitative. Helium or other gas carries the sample along a thin tube (column) packed with silica. A computer displays which compounds, and how much, are in the mixture.

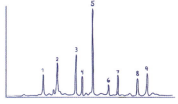

Gas chromatography detects banned substances in an athlete's urine.

The peaks on this chromatogram show nine compounds in peppermint oil.

Volumetric titration

Titration is quantitative. The amount of reagent needed to complete a reaction shows how concentrated a substance is.

Volumetric titration of an acid-alkali neutralization.

A burette is used to measure how much reagent is added to a solution.

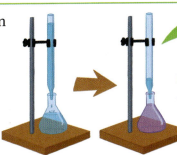

INDICATORS: PAGE 16

Indicator changes color when the right amount of reagent has been added.

Testing for gases

A splint is a thin piece of wood that can be lit and blown out, so it glows.

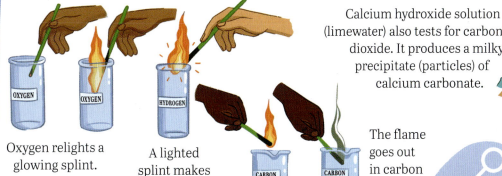

Oxygen relights a glowing splint.

A lighted splint makes hydrogen pop!

The flame goes out in carbon dioxide.

Calcium hydroxide solution (limewater) also tests for carbon dioxide. It produces a milky precipitate (particles) of calcium carbonate.

RESPIRATION: PAGE 68

Flame tests

The ions in some metal salts produce amazing colors when heated.

REACTIONS OF METALS: PAGE 43

Some metals' flame colors are:

Barium
Strontium
Lithium
Sodium
Copper
Potassium

Metal compounds make fireworks colorful.

Spectroscopy

Spectroscopy identifies chemicals from the light waves they absorb, emit (produce), or reflect.

The absorption and emission spectra of a chemical are opposites.

An infrared spectrometer uses infrared light. It's used to detect illegal substances.

Crystallography

X-ray crystallography shows the structures of molecules.

SEEING ATOMS AND MOLECULES: PAGE 60

53

Inorganic chemistry

Inorganic chemistry is all about chemicals that are not carbon-based compounds. There are over 100,000 inorganic compounds. They include minerals, metals, and ceramics.

BRANCHES OF CHEMISTRY: PAGE 8

Inorganic chemicals are one of the major branches of chemistry.

Their molecules don't contain carbon-hydrogen bonds. They occur naturally in Earth's atmosphere, and as minerals and metals in rocks and soil.

Inorganic compounds have many uses. Fuels, fertilizers, explosives, catalysts, coatings, surfactants, and medicines are just a few. They often have high melting points and useful conducting or insulating properties.

Compounds of carbon, titanium, cobalt, chromium, and cadmium make paint pigments.

Carbon black

Titanium white

Cobalt violet

Cobalt blue

Chrome green

Cadmium orange

Cadmium red

Two other important inorganic compounds are sodium chloride and ammonia.

SULFURIC ACID: PAGE 51

The most important inorganic chemical, with the greatest volume produced in the world, is sulfuric acid

Sodium chloride

Worldwide, 294 million metric tons (324 million tons) of sodium chloride (NaCl) was mined in 2022, from rock salt and brines. NaCl is used to obtain chlorine and sodium hydroxide—and turned into many more chemicals, including sodium carbonate (soda ash), sodium sulfate, and hydrochloric acid.

Sodium chloride is food salt, and it's used to deice roads.

Salt mining leaves huge caverns, sometimes used as storage space.

CHLOR-ALKALI PROCESS: PAGE 59

Ammonia

World ammonia (NH_3) manufacturing was around 183 million metric tons (202 million tons) in 2022. Over half of production goes into nitrogen fertilizers and agrochemicals. It has many uses, including explosives, plastics, fuels, dyes, medicines, and textiles.

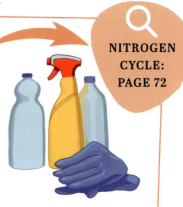

Ammonia is transported by train, road, or sea.

Ammonia is an important cleaning agent.

NITROGEN CYCLE: PAGE 72

Minerals

Minerals are natural, crystalline, inorganic solids. Metal ores and naturally pure metals, like gold, are minerals, as are pebbles and gemstones, such as rubies. Diamond is pure crystalline carbon, so it's a mineral, too.

Other examples are sand, limestone (calcium carbonate), and clays such as kaolin.

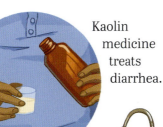

Kaolin medicine treats diarrhea.

Magnetite is a magnetic iron ore, used to make steel and in catalysts and pigments.

Landscapes like Rainbow Mountain in Peru display colorful minerals.

Metals

Metals have properties that make them very useful, from construction to electronics.

Steel (a metal) and granite (a mineral) work together in constructions from bridges to kitchens.

All our electronics devices depend on metals and semi-metals.

METALS: PAGE 42

SEMI-METALS: PAGE 44

Ceramics

Ceramics are materials that include glass, china, and porcelain, made from inorganic compounds. Porcelain is made from kaolin with other minerals, heated to 1,400 °C (2,600 °F).

Pottery is a type of ceramic.

Making glass

When sand (silicon dioxide, or silica) is melted at around 1,700 °C (3,090 °F), it cools with a new, amorphous (noncrystalline) structure. It forms glass—a useful, cheap, transparent material that's easy to shape when molten.

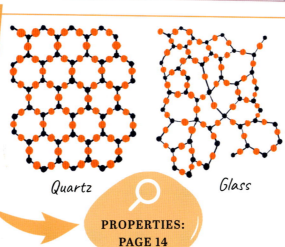

Quartz

Glass

Quartz, a crystalline silica, has a covalent lattice structure. The amorphous structure of glass is messier!

Pigments add color to stained glass windows.

LATTICES: PAGE 27

PROPERTIES: PAGE 14

Organic chemistry

Organic chemistry involves molecules that contain carbon, usually with carbon-hydrogen bonds. There are millions of organic compounds. The chemicals that make life possible are organic.

Carbon's unique way of making covalent bonds in chains and rings creates a huge range of organic chemicals. Hydrocarbons—just carbon and hydrogen—are the simplest.

Organic chemicals containing other atoms, especially oxygen and nitrogen, make up the molecules of living bodies.

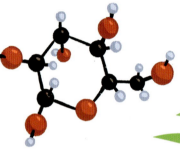

Glucose is a simple sugar with the chemical formula $C_6H_{12}O_6$

COMPOUNDS: PAGE 24

CHEMICAL FORMULAE: PAGE 26

GLUCOSE: PAGE 74

Molecules in a homologous series have a functional group of atoms that gives them their properties.

Friedrich Wöhler

Before 1828, scientists believed that organic chemicals had a special "life force." Friedrich Wöhler proved them wrong when he produced urea (previously found in urine) from an inorganic compound.

Urea is a nitrogen fertilizer for crops such as cotton.

Crude oil and natural gas are the remains of living things. They are raw materials for organic chemicals called petrochemicals.

A separate use of the word "organic" means food produced without synthetic chemicals.

Homologous series

A homologous series is organic molecules with similar structure and formulae. Each molecule has one carbon and two hydrogen atoms more than the one before. Homologous series show trends in their properties.

Two homologous series are **alkanes** and **alkenes**. They are volatile chemicals—they have low boiling points that get higher as the molecules get bigger.

FRACTIONAL DISTILLATION: PAGE 50

FOOD CHEMICALS: PAGE 78

Alcohols

Alcohols are colorless liquids that burn with a blue flame. They always have a hydrogen and oxygen atom group (-OH).

Methanol, ethanol, and propanol are used as fuels and solvents.

Methanol (CH$_3$OH)

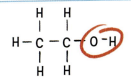
Ethanol (C$_2$H$_5$OH)

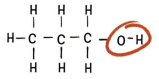
Propanol (C$_3$H$_7$OH)

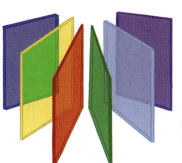

Methanol is an important feedstock for acrylic plastics.

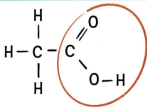

Ethanol is found in alcoholic drinks and fermenting, rotting fruit.

FERMENTATION: PAGE 69

Carboxylic acids

Carboxylic acids are weak acids. They contain a -COOH group.

Ethanoic acid (CH$_3$COOH)

Vinegar is dilute ethanoic acid (also called acetic acid).

ACIDS: PAGE 16

Amino acids

Amino acids contain functional groups with nitrogen atoms. They are monomers (small molecules) for proteins.

Foods rich in amino acids, such as nuts, help us build healthy bodies.

BODY BIOCHEMISTRY: PAGE 76–77

Organometallic compounds

Organometals have bonds between a carbon atom and a metal. They are catalysts.

CATALYSTS: PAGE 33

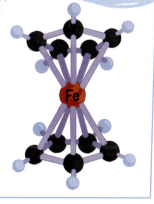

Ferrocene (C$_{10}$H$_{10}$Fe) is an antiknock agent in petrol.

Alkanes and alkenes

Alkane molecules are saturated—all bonds are single bonds.

The first four alkanes are methane (CH$_4$), ethane (C$_2$H$_6$), propane (C$_3$H$_8$), and butane (C$_4$H$_{10}$)

Alkene molecules contain a double bond—they are unsaturated.

The first three alkenes are ethylene (C$_2$H$_4$), propene (C$_3$H$_6$), and butene (C$_4$H$_8$).

Small unsaturated molecules are monomers. They polymerize (join up) to form long-chain polymers.

DOUBLE BONDS: PAGE 28

POLYMERS: PAGE 89

57

Electrochemistry

Many chemical reactions involve electrical energy. It's produced in some reactions and used in others. The study and use of electrical energy in chemical reactions is electrochemistry.

Electrical energy comes from a flow of charged particles—electrons or ions.

Lightning is a sudden burst of electrical energy.

When electrical energy is converted to chemical energy, or the other way around, that is electrochemistry.

ELECTRONS:
PAGE 21

THE LAW OF
CONSERVATION
OF ENERGY:
PAGE 32

Electrolysis has important industrial uses.

Electricity

The electricity industry generates electrical energy from other forms of energy. It makes electricity flow through wires in a closed circuit. This makes an electric current, which powers our electrical devices.

ELECTRICAL
CONDUCTORS:
PAGE 83

Batteries

A battery is an electrochemical cell. It stores chemical energy and converts it to electrical energy. It contains an electrolyte—a compound containing ions—and two electrodes made of different metals. Electrons cross the electrolyte between the electrodes, forming a circuit.

A lemon battery lights a bulb because citric acid in the juice carries the charge and completes the circuit.

A fuel cell uses chemical energy from hydrogen or a hydrocarbon fuel. The fuel reacts with oxygen to produce electricity.

The UK's first hydrogen powered passenger ferry was built in 2010.

Electrolytic cell

Electrolysis converts electrical into chemical energy. In an electrolytic cell, the electrolyte molecules split (decompose), producing positive and negative charged particles that move toward opposite electrodes.

Positive electrode

Battery

Negative electrode

Negative ions

Positive ions

Electrolyte

A battery supplies electrical energy in an electrolytic cell.

THERMAL
DECOMPOSITION:
PAGE 31

Metals extraction

Electrolysis separates metals, such as sodium, from their compounds. Solid sodium chloride (NaCl) can't conduct electricity, but molten (melted) NaCl can, because the charged particles are free to move apart.

In electrolysis of molten NaCl, pure sodium gathers on one electrode, and chlorine gas on the other.

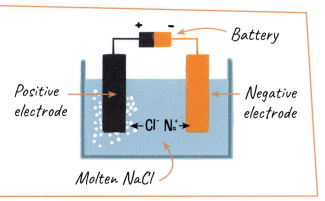

Battery

Positive electrode

Negative electrode

← Cl⁻ Na⁺ →

Molten NaCl

Chlor-alkali process

Electrolysis of sodium chloride (NaCl) solution breaks down the NaCl and the water molecules to produce sodium hydroxide, chlorine, and hydrogen. This chlor-alkali process is the most important industrial use of electrochemistry.

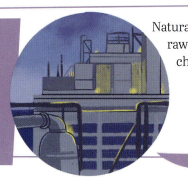

Natural brines are the raw materials for chlor-alkali plants.

INDUSTRIAL CHEMISTRY: PAGE 50

Splitting water

Electrolysis splits water molecules into hydrogen and oxygen. The hydrogen can be used as fuel—but it's expensive and not totally environmentally friendly because it needs electricity.

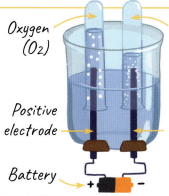

Oxygen (O₂)

Hydrogen (H₂)

Positive electrode

Negative electrode

Battery

Astronauts on the International Space Station breathe oxygen from electrolysis of water.

Never try putting electricity near water—it's very dangerous.

Electroplating

Electrolysis coats metals with another metal. It can give a shiny silver-plating to objects made of dull nickel.

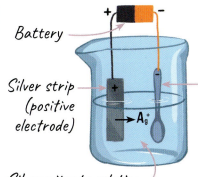

Battery

Silver moves from the silver electrode to coat the spoon.

Silver strip (positive electrode)

Nickel spoon (negative electrode)

→ Ag⁺

Silver nitrate solution

Galvanizing

Galvanizing is electroplating with zinc. Iron-based metals get rusty. A zinc coating protects them from corrosion.

Crystals of zinc form on galvanized steel objects.

CORROSION: PAGE 31

Writer Mary Shelley created the character of Frankenstein's monster in 1818, after hearing about electrochemistry.

59

Seeing atoms and molecules

Around 500,000 atoms fit on the cut edge of a sheet of paper. People have been trying to find ways to look at these tiny structures for over a hundred years.

Scientists now have techniques to see molecules and detect the presence of atoms, or even to see actual atoms.

Nuclear magnetic resonance (NMR) spectroscopy can examine molecules in living tissues.

Artificial intelligence uses NMR to build complex models of molecules, like this protein, calmodulin.

Microscopes magnify—make things look bigger. The latest microscopes have much greater magnification and resolution (detail) than traditional optical (light) microscopes.

MOLECULES: PAGE 26

SPECTROSCOPY: PAGE 53

X-ray crystallography

X-ray crystallography lets us see atoms indirectly, in crystals, or crystallized materials. X-rays passing through a crystal diffract—they bounce off the atoms and spread out. The scattered X-rays make a photographic image, and the pattern shows how the atoms are arranged in the crystal.

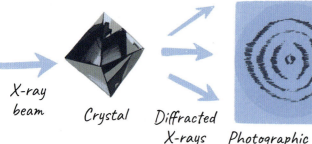

X-ray beam · Crystal · Diffracted X-rays · Photographic image

The X-ray diffraction pattern made by DNA in 1953 showed that the molecule is a double helix (spiral).

Modern crystallography uses intense X-rays emitted inside particle accelerators like the 27-km (17-mile) Large Hadron Collider in Europe.

DNA: PAGE 76

MORE

Nanotechnology

Crystallography helps nanotechnologists develop and study ultrathin nanomaterials. Nanomaterials contain nanoparticles no more than 100 nm long.

Nanomaterials' high surface area and other unusual properties make them useful in semiconductors, water purification, drug delivery systems, sensors, catalysts, and composites.

A nanometer (nm) is a billionth of a meter (m)—that's a millionth of a millimeter (mm).

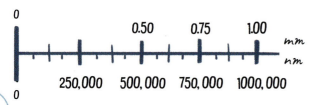

	0		0.50	0.75	1.00	mm
0		250,000	500,000	750,000	1000,000	nm

Some nanomaterials—such as carbon fullerenes and graphene—are just one carbon atom thick.

Graphene · Fullerene

COMPOSITES: PAGE 80

Optical microscopes

Optical microscopes pass light through glass lenses. They can make an object look 2,000 times larger than actual size, but they can never show anything smaller than 200 nm.

A light microscope shows objects the size of blood cells and bacteria.

CHEMISTRY IN MEDICINE: PAGE 84

Electron microscopes

Electron microscopes can detect objects as small as 0.05 nm. A beam of electrons passes through a sample, and a computer creates an image. Electron microscopes can show us nanoparticles, viruses, and molecules, but they can't show atoms in detail.

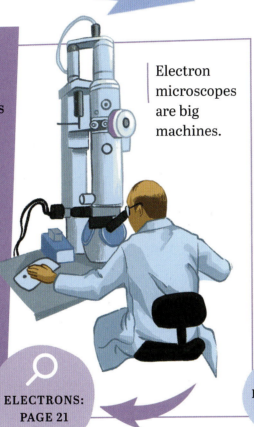

Electron microscopes are big machines.

ELECTRONS: PAGE 21

Electron ptychography

Electron ptychography improves the resolution in electron microscopy and produces 3D pictures of atoms.

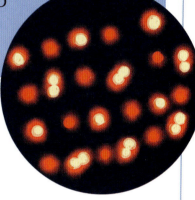

In 2021, scientists at Cornell University, Ithaca, New York, USA, created an image of atoms in a praseodymium crystal, magnified 100 million times.

PRASEODYMIUM: PAGE 36

Scanning probe microscopes

Scanning probe microscopes have a tiny needle (probe), just one atom wide. It moves over the surface of a sample, "feeling" the atoms, and a computer creates an image.

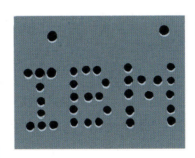

In 1989, workers at IBM used a scanning probe microscope to spell their company name with 35 atoms of the element xenon. The letters are 5 nm tall.

XENON: PAGE 41

WHAT IS AN ATOM?: PAGE 20

The Universe

Stars are chemical factories. The Universe is made of atoms forged in burning stars, or in the explosive deaths of stars, or even before stars ignite.

Stars make atoms and produce energy—heat and light. They have been fusing hydrogen nuclei and making helium since the first ones burst into light, over 13 billion years ago.

Helium and other nuclei fuse to make heavier elements. All the elements, apart from a few human-made giant atoms, are created by nuclear reactions in space.

WHAT IS AN ATOM?: PAGE 20

THE LIGHTEST ELEMENTS: PAGE 38

THE HEAVIEST ELEMENTS: PAGE 46

Stars start to grow as protostars in nebulae. They start making helium and make larger elements as they age.

Astronomers use spectroscopes to detect elements in stars.

The core of stars are furnaces, where nuclei collide and fuse. The light they produce travels out from the hot core. Atoms in the star's cooler atmosphere absorb some wavelengths, making a "fingerprint" on the spectrum.

SPECTROSCOPY: PAGE 53

Cooler outer layers

Our Sun's absorption spectrum shows it is mainly hydrogen and helium.

Sun's core

Nebulae and protostars

Nebulae are clouds of dust and hydrogen. In a "star nursery" nebula, areas of matter collapse under gravity, heat up, and form protostars.

The horsehead nebula is 1,600 light-years* away from Earth.

*A light-year is the distance light travels in one year—about 9 trillion km (over 6 trillion miles).

CHEMICALS, MATTER, AND MATERIALS: PAGE 6

Stars

A protostar becomes a star when it gets so hot that it starts fusing hydrogen, producing helium and huge amounts of energy.

Sunshine is heat and light from hydrogen fusion.

Red giants

When the star runs out of hydrogen, it swells. It becomes a red giant and starts fusing helium to make carbon. Colossal "super" red giants produce all the elements up to iron.

Our Sun will become a red giant in 5 billion years. Stars eight times heavier become super red giants.

Red giant

Super red giant

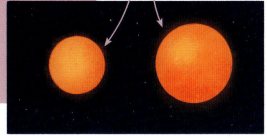

Neutron absorption

Elements heavier than iron are forged when nuclei absorb neutrons. This happens in supernovae, and when neutron stars** collide.

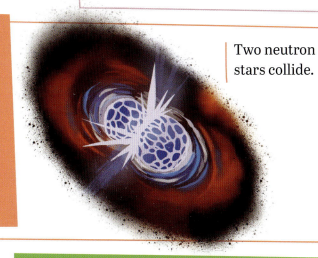

Two neutron stars collide.

**Neutron stars and black holes are formed by supernova explosions.

Supernovae

Super red giants become supernovae, finally exploding and flinging all their atoms into space.

Supernova 1987A is 170,000 light-years away. Images show rings of ejected matter.

Thin matter

Matter is thinly spread between stars in galaxies. This "thin matter" eventually forms new solar systems, and the atoms become part of new stars and planets—and life.

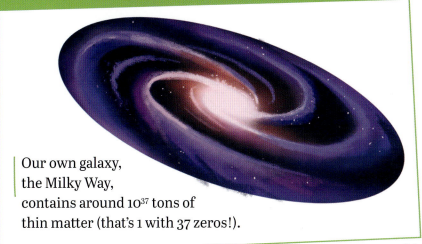

Our own galaxy, the Milky Way, contains around 10^{37} tons of thin matter (that's 1 with 37 zeros!).

Our world

The chemicals in Earth's rocks, air, and oceans explain how it supports life, and why it's the perfect distance from the Sun.

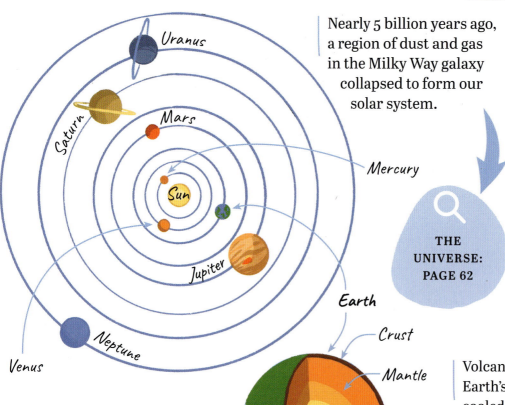

Nearly 5 billion years ago, a region of dust and gas in the Milky Way galaxy collapsed to form our solar system.

THE UNIVERSE: PAGE 62
THE UNIVERSE: PAGE 62

Early Earth had the right elements to form a metallic core, a semi-molten mantle, a rocky surface crust, and life-supporting atmosphere.

The young Earth's hot, molten materials separated. Heavier elements sank, and lighter materials drifted up and cooled.

Volcanic gases began to form Earth's atmosphere. When it cooled, it began to rain. Earth was just the right distance from the Sun for liquid water to gather in oceans—making life possible.

WATER: PAGE 66

MORE

Plate Tectonics

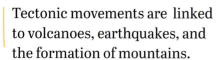

Earth's crust is made of plates that move very slowly—plate tectonics.

Tectonic movements are linked to volcanoes, earthquakes, and the formation of mountains.

The highest mountain in the world grows around 4 mm (0.12 inches) a year.

Rock cycle

Weather erodes surface rocks. Rivers carry the pieces to the sea to form sediments. The sediments get squashed and become sedimentary rocks. Underground heat and pressure change them into metamorphic rocks. They melt and come to the surface as volcanic magma, which cools as igneous rocks. The cycle continues.

Core

The core is 85% iron, 10% nickel, and 5% silicon. The inner core is solid, and the outer core is liquid. The molten metal flows as the Earth spins, causing a magnetic field that shields us from dangerous solar winds.

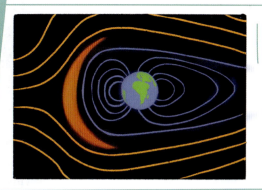

It is the magnetic field that gives us the points of the compass.

Mantle

The mantle is a thick layer of magma—hot, slowly flowing semi-molten rock.

Currents of flowing magma in the mantle affect crustal movements.

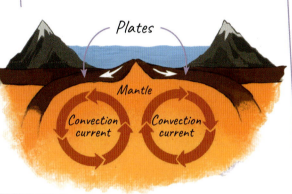

Plates

Mantle

Convection current

Convection current

Crust

The crust is mainly oxygen and silicon. These elements with other nonmetals and metals form silicate and oxide minerals, which make Earth's rocks and ores.

The crust is thin—no more than 70 km (44 miles) thick—like the skin of an apple.

Atmosphere

The air we breathe at the bottom of the atmosphere is 78% nitrogen and 21% oxygen. Argon, water, carbon dioxide, and other gases make up only 1%. The atmosphere protects Earth from radiation and keeps it warm.

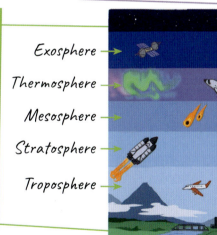

Exosphere

Thermosphere

Mesosphere

Stratosphere

Troposphere

Charged particles from the Sun create aurora lights in the thermosphere.

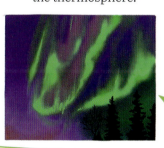

BREATHING:
PAGE 68

GREENHOUSE
EFFECT:
PAGE 70

ENERGY,
RESOURCES,
AND
RECYCLING:
PAGE 90

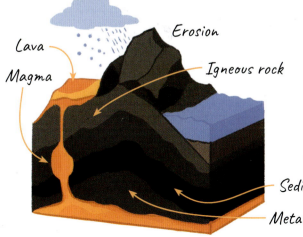

Lava

Magma

Erosion

Igneous rock

Sedimentary rock

Metamorphic rock

Sedimentary limestone often contains fossils—the remains of long-dead creatures.

Layers of plant and animal remains form fossil fuels.

Water

Water can be a hot drink, an ice cube, or vapor in the air. We regularly see it in all three states—and that makes water special.

Water (H_2O) is an unusual compound because it exists at normal temperatures as liquid, solid, and gas.

COMPOUNDS: PAGE 24

MOLECULES: PAGE 26

Water is special because it has very odd properties.

OUR WORLD: PAGE 64

Water on Earth

Liquid and frozen water cover around 75% of Earth's surface.

Ice keeps the planet cool by reflecting heat back into space, and it keeps the sea warm because it insulates water underneath.

INSULATING: PAGE 15

CHANGING STATES: PAGE 11

The water cycle

Water is constantly cycled through the environment. Liquid water evaporates. The vapor cools in the air and condenses into water droplets in clouds. The droplets get heavier and fall as precipitation—rain, snow, or hail. Water that falls on land runs over the surface or moves through the ground. It passes into, and out of, plants and animals.

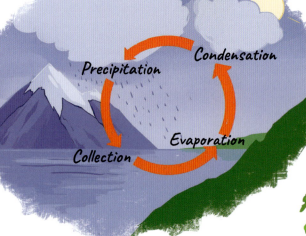

Condensation

Precipitation

Collection

Evaporation

Water collects in the oceans, and the cycle goes on.

Living things

Living things need water for all the reactions happening in their cells.

A 116 m- (380 ft-) tall redwood tree may lift around 1,890 l (500 gal) of water from its roots to its top every day.

PHOTOSYNTHESIS AND RESPIRATION: PAGE 68

BODY BIOCHEMISTRY: PAGE 76

Solid water floats

Water expands when it freezes. Its molecules crystallize into rings in a lattice. Extra space in the rings makes the solid less dense—so ice floats.

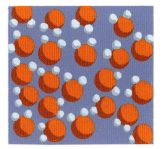

Liquid water

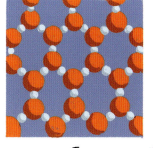

Ice

LATTICES: PAGE 27

Water sticks to itself

Water molecules stick together. This is "cohesion." It creates high surface tension, which can keep an overfull glass of water from spilling.

Surface tension

Pond skaters, or water striders, use the high surface tension to walk on water.

Water sticks to other things

Water molecules stick to other substances. This is "adhesion."

Raindrops stick to window glass and spiderwebs by adhesion.

Water defies gravity

Plants can move water up thin tubes against gravity, because the sticky molecules are pulled up by water evaporating from the topmost leaves.

Dyes show the tubes in a celery stalk.

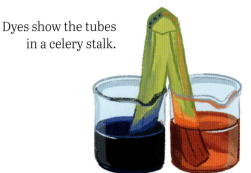

Water is an excellent solvent

Water dissolves many substances.

Seawater dissolves salts from rocks, and it stores carbon by dissolving and absorbing CO_2 from the atmosphere.

CLIMATE CHANGE: PAGE 70

DISSOLVING: PAGE 12

Photosynthesis and respiration

Being alive takes energy—and that comes from the Sun. Plants trap solar energy, which flows through the food chain and becomes energy for animals.

Photosynthesis captures sunlight and stores it as chemical energy in a sugar (glucose $C_6H_{12}O_6$). Oxygen (O_2) is produced, which plants and animals use in respiration.

Respiration turns chemical energy into energy for living processes. It breaks down glucose into carbon dioxide (CO_2), which plants use in photosynthesis.

The two reactions cycle oxygen, carbon, and water (H_2O) through the environment. They help keep oxygen and CO_2 levels in the air steady.

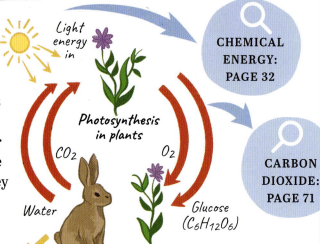

Light energy in

Photosynthesis in plants

CO_2

O_2

Water

Glucose ($C_6H_{12}O_6$)

Energy out

Respiration in plants and animals

CHEMICAL ENERGY: PAGE 32

CARBON DIOXIDE: PAGE 71

ENDOTHERMIC AND EXOTHERMIC: PAGE 32

Photosynthesis

Plants absorb carbon dioxide from the air, and water from the soil for photosynthesis. The reaction is endothermic.

The word equation is:

Carbon dioxide + water + energy → glucose + oxygen

Some glucose gives the plant immediate energy, and some is turned into larger molecules, such as starch and cellulose.

CO_2

O_2

Glucose ($C_6H_{12}O_6$)

Water

EQUATIONS: PAGE 30

Respiration

Respiration is exothermic. Most respiration is aerobic—it needs oxygen.

Aerobic respiration is the opposite of photosynthesis. The word equation is:

Glucose + oxygen → carbon dioxide + water + energy

Thinking uses a lot of energy!

Plants respire, but they don't breathe! Breathing is when we move air into our lungs to get oxygen, and out again to expel CO_2 and water. Blood carries oxygen to body cells for respiration.

PLANT BIOCHEMISTRY: PAGE 74

Photosynthesis and respiration are both metabolic processes in living cells.

Food chain

Energy captured by photosynthesis enters the food chain when animals eat plants.

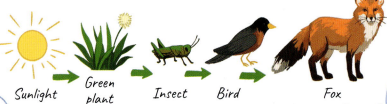

Sunlight

Green plant

Insect

Bird

Fox

BODY BIOCHEMISTRY: PAGE 76

Chemosynthesis

A few organisms use energy from chemical reactions, instead of sunlight, to build food molecules.

Snottites support food chains that include cave-living fish.

SNOTTITES: PAGE 45

Anaerobic respiration

Respiration that happens without oxygen is anaerobic.

Fermentation, such as by yeasts in beer-making, is anaerobic respiration.

Glucose → carbon dioxide + ethanol + energy

Anaerobic respiration helps our muscles keep going during hard exercise. It produces lactic acid, which breaks down after we stop running:

Glucose → lactic acid + energy

Cells

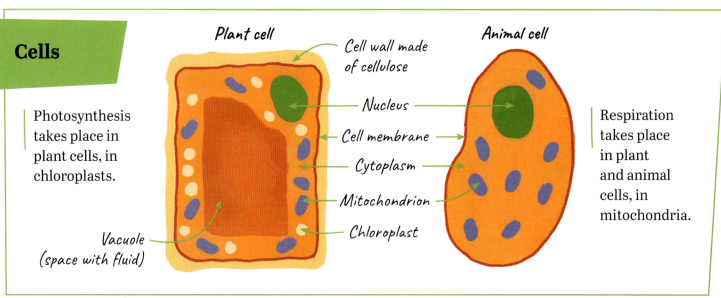

Plant cell

Animal cell

Cell wall made of cellulose

Nucleus

Cell membrane

Cytoplasm

Mitochondrion

Chloroplast

Vacuole (space with fluid)

Photosynthesis takes place in plant cells, in chloroplasts.

Respiration takes place in plant and animal cells, in mitochondria.

Cell structures

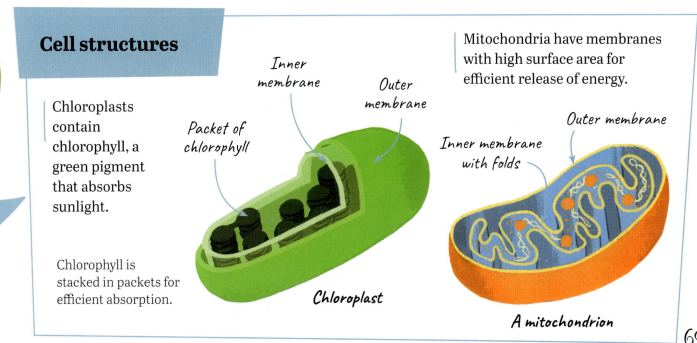

Mitochondria have membranes with high surface area for efficient release of energy.

Chloroplasts contain chlorophyll, a green pigment that absorbs sunlight.

Chlorophyll is stacked in packets for efficient absorption.

Inner membrane

Outer membrane

Packet of chlorophyll

Chloroplast

Inner membrane with folds

Outer membrane

A mitochondrion

Climate change

Electricity and manufactured goods make our lives comfortable, but there's a downside—industry produces pollutants that damage the environment and cause climate change.

Over the last 200 years, people have developed machines for power generation, mining, manufacturing, agriculture, and transportation.

Modern industry produces more of everything, but it also produces more waste, such as plastics, and releases harmful chemicals including greenhouse gases that affect the climate.

Farming was hard work before the Industrial Revolution.

PLASTIC: PAGE 89

Carbon dioxide, methane, nitrous oxide, and CFCs are all greenhouse gases.

Weather and climate

Weather—whether it's raining or sunny outside—changes from day to day. Climate is the pattern of temperature and rainfall seen over many years. The world has different climate zones.

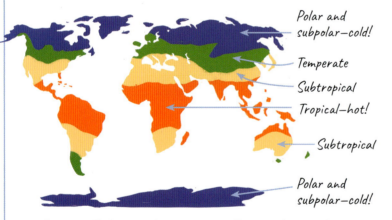

Polar and subpolar—cold!

Temperate

Subtropical

Tropical—hot!

Subtropical

Polar and subpolar—cold!

Earth's overall climate changes naturally over thousands of years—but now it's changing faster than expected.

The greenhouse effect

Gases in Earth's atmosphere trap some of the sun's energy, keeping the planet warm. This is the "greenhouse effect." But industry releases more greenhouse gases into the atmosphere, causing Earth to warm up too quickly—global warming.

Global warming raises sea levels and causes extreme weather. It can destroy human homes and wildlife habitats, and even make species extinct.

MORE

Acid rain and acidic oceans

Burning fossil fuels emits several oxide gases—sulfur dioxide, nitrogen oxides, and CO_2. They dissolve in water, making "acid rain," which harms plants, damages buildings, and increases ocean acidity.

Acidic oceans damage coral reefs, causing bleaching.

ACIDS: PAGE 16

Carbon dioxide

Carbon dioxide (CO_2) is a normal part of the atmosphere, but it also makes up 75% of greenhouse gases emitted by human activities. Ten percent of CO_2 emissions come from vehicles.

PHOTOSYNTHESIS: PAGE 68

ENERGY, RESOURCES, AND RECYCLING: PAGE 90

COMBUSTION: PAGE 31

INDUSTRIAL CHEMISTRY: PAGE 50

Methane

Methane (CH_4) occurs naturally, released from decaying organic matter. Extra methane comes from landfill waste, fossil fuels, and farm animals.

Landfill methane can be converted into electricity.

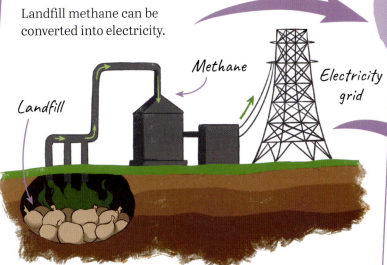

Methane

Landfill

Electricity grid

METHANE: PAGE 26

ORGANIC CHEMISTRY: PAGE 56

Nitrous oxide

Nitrous oxide (N_2O) is a greenhouse gas 300 times stronger than CO_2. It's released from power plants, wastewater treatment, and agricultural industries.

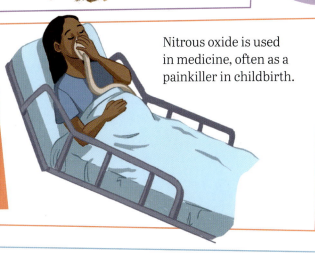

Nitrous oxide is used in medicine, often as a painkiller in childbirth.

Chlorofluorocarbons (CFCs)

Made by humans, CFCs are gases containing carbon, chlorine, and fluorine, once used in aerosols and refrigerators. They are now mostly banned, but they stay in the atmosphere for many years. CFCs damage the atmosphere's ozone (O_3) layer, which protects us from harmful radiation.

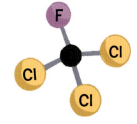

Trichlorofluoromethane (CCl_3F), or CFC-11, was a commonly emitted CFC.

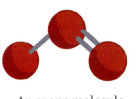

An ozone molecule contains three oxygen atoms.

Nitrogen cycle

Nitrogen is common, and all living things need it—but there's a problem. It's an unreactive gas and doesn't easily make compounds, so it's difficult to get from the atmosphere.

Earth's atmosphere is 78% nitrogen (N_2). The N_2 molecule is unreactive because the two atoms are joined by a triple covalent bond.

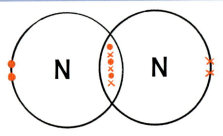

The triple bond is very hard to break.

SINGLE, DOUBLE, AND TRIPLE BONDS: PAGE 28

The nitrogen cycle

Before nitrogen can enter plants and the food chain, the N_2 molecules must be pulled apart. Nitrogen-fixing bacteria do this. The separated atoms then form compounds that plant roots can absorb. The flow of nitrogen through the environment is the nitrogen cycle.

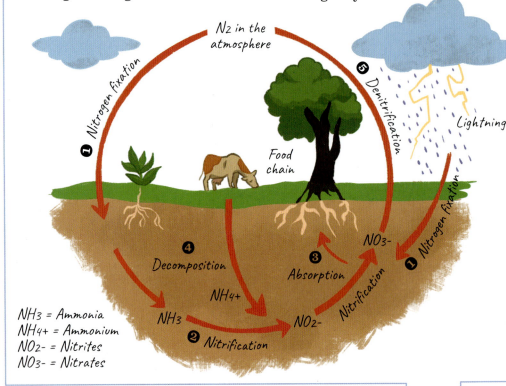

N_2 in the atmosphere

① Nitrogen fixation

⑤ Denitrification

Lightning

Food chain

④ Decomposition

③ Absorption

NO_3-

① Nitrogen fixation

Nitrification

NH_4+

NH_3

NO_2-

② Nitrification

NH_3 = Ammonia
NH_4+ = Ammonium
NO_2- = Nitrites
NO_3- = Nitrates

Microorganisms play a part in all stages of the nitrogen cycle:

- nitrogen fixation
- nitrification
- absorption
- decomposition
- denitrification

FERTILIZERS: PAGE 86

MORE

Haber process

Nitrogen is a nonmetal and an important industrial chemical.

It's used in the Haber process, which fixes N_2 by a reaction with hydrogen to make ammonia.

Ammonia is used to make nitric acid, and ammonia and nitric acid together make ammonium nitrate fertilizer.

Fertilizers help farmers grow enough food, but overuse of fertilizers can upset the nitrogen cycle and cause pollution.

Rivers polluted by nitrates can quickly become clogged with algae.

NONMETALS: PAGE 44

INDUSTRIAL CHEMISTRY: PAGE 50

REACTIONS: PAGE 30

1 Nitrogen fixation

Nitrogen-fixing soil bacteria live on nodules (swellings) on the roots of legumes (pealike plants). They "fix" nitrogen—break its molecules so it can react to make ammonia and other compunds.

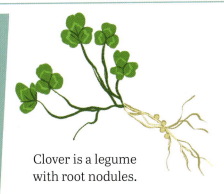

Clover is a legume with root nodules.

Lightning and volcanoes also fix atmospheric nitrogen.

2 Nitrification

Nitrifying bacteria in soil convert ammonia and ammonium compounds into nitrite and nitrate compounds.

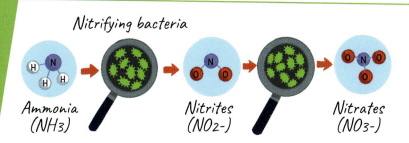

Nitrifying bacteria

Ammonia (NH_3)　Nitrites (NO_2-)　Nitrates (NO_3-)

3 Absorption

Plants absorb nitrates and use the nitrogen in their bodies.

BODY BIO-CHEMISTRY: PAGE 76

METHANE: PAGE 71

Animals absorb nitrogen from their food.*

Wheat plants with too little nitrogen have smaller, yellow leaves.

* Gut microbes produce some methane!

5 Denitrification

Denitrifying bacteria in soil turn some nitrates into nitrogen (N_2) gas, which reenters the atmosphere.

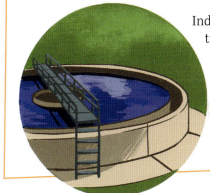

Industrial wastewater treatment also uses denitrifying bacteria to turn nitrates into nitrogen gas.

4 Decomposition

Decomposers—fungi and bacteria—break down organic waste into ammonium (NH_4+) compounds.

Insects like dung beetles help recycle nitrogen and other nutrients in animal waste.

Plant biochemistry

Plants are the foundation of food chains. They are biochemical factories, reacting with chemicals to build molecules that then pass to animals.

Glucose, the sugar made by photosynthesis, is used to release energy for metabolism—all the biochemical processes that happen in living cells to keep organisms alive.

Plants also use glucose for building larger biomolecules.*

PHOTOSYNTHESIS AND RESPIRATION: PAGE 68

ORGANIC CHEMISTRY: PAGE 56

POLYMERS: PAGE 88

As well as for energy and food, plants use chemicals for response, defense, and communication.

Cellulose and starch

Sugars, cellulose, and starch are carbohydrates—they contain carbon, hydrogen, and oxygen.

Cellulose and starch are biopolymers made from repeating units. Their monomer is glucose.

Other biomolecules

Plants also make lipids (fats and oils), proteins, and DNA to build their bodies.

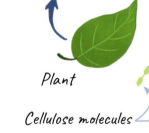

Plant cells

Cell walls

Cellulose fibers

Plant

Cellulose molecules

Bundles of cellulose molecules

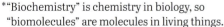

Cellulose is unbranched chains of glucose. It makes strong cell walls to stiffen the plant.

Starch

Starch is branching chains of glucose molecules. It stores energy in structures such as potatoes.

DNA in seeds holds the information for growing into an adult plant.

*"Biochemistry" is chemistry in biology, so "biomolecules" are molecules in living things.

MORE

DNA: PAGE 76

Enzymes

Enzymes break down chemicals in metabolism. They fit their target molecules like a lock and key.

Enzyme names end in **-ase**. Amylase breaks down starch into glucose for energy.

Fungi have cellulase to digest cellulose in dead wood.

CATALYSTS: PAGE 33

Response

Auxins are hormones—chemical messengers. They help plants grow in response to light and gravity.

Auxins move through shoots and roots by diffusion. Higher concentrations make shoot cells grow faster and root cells grow more slowly.

Shoots grow toward light.

Shaded cells grow faster and bigger

Auxin diffuses to the shaded side of shoot

Light

Shoot

Roots grow toward gravity.

CONCENTRATION: PAGE 12

The roots of a toppled plant bend downward, and the shoot bends upward.

Ethene is a plant hormone that controls ripening in fruit.

ETHYLENE: PAGE 27

Defense

Irritants or poisons protect plants by putting off, or killing, pests.

Mint releases chemicals that taste bad to insects.

Some chemicals fight disease.

Salicylic acid protects willow trees from bacteria and fungi.

It's also the active ingredient in aspirin.

CHEMISTRY IN MEDICINE: PAGE 84

Communication

Trees communicate with each other through the "wood wide web." A network of fungal threads lets trees share glucose with "friends"—and send harmful chemicals to discourage other neighbors.

The underground threads of toadstools connect the roots of trees.

Body biochemistry

Humans and other animals can't capture the sun's energy to make molecules, like plants do. Instead, they get chemicals from the food chain.

Food chains begin with plant photosynthesis.

By eating plants or other animals, we absorb the nutrients we need for metabolism.

Our digestive systems break down nutrients into smaller molecules, such as glucose and amino acids.

PLANT BIOCHEMISTRY: PAGE 74

PHOTOSYNTHESIS: PAGE 68

The small molecules are absorbed and transported in the blood to body cells. There, respiration releases energy, and chemical reactions build new biomolecules, including our own DNA and proteins.

FOOD CHEMICALS: PAGE 78

Others

Fats

Protein around 20%

Water around 60%;

Apart from water and fat, the human body is mostly protein. Muscles, hormones, and enzymes (biological catalysts) are all proteins.

AMINO ACIDS: PAGE 57

Different animal groups build very different bodies. Skeletons give animals shape, protect them, let them move, and act as tools or weapons. Skeletons can be inside or outside the body, and made of a variety of materials.

CATALYSTS: PAGE 33

RESPIRATION: PAGE 68

MORE

DNA

DNA (deoxyribonucleic acid) carries the inherited genetic code for making proteins. All animal and plant cells have copies of it.

Sugar-phosphate backbone

Bases

The genetic code is in the sequence of bases.

Skin color is a characteristic passed on in genes.

DNA is shaped like a long, spiral ladder—a double helix. It's a biopolymer, and its monomers are nucleotides. Nucleotides contain bases (nitrogen-containing compounds).

POLYMERS: PAGE 88

A double chain of nucleotides makes a DNA molecule, with the bases—❶ Adenine, ❷ thymine, ❸ guanine, and ❹ cytosine—forming the rungs of the "ladder."

A person has at least 20,000 genes—and one gene may be hundreds of thousands of nucleotides—so DNA molecules are very long!

Bones

Backboned animals like humans have inside skeletons, with bones made of collagen (a protein) hardened by calcium phosphate.

X-ray

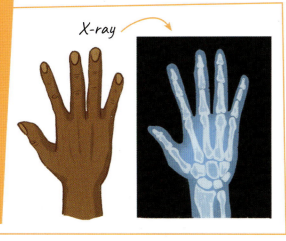

Chitin

Insects and crustaceans like crabs have outside "exoskeletons" made of chitin—a carbohydrate.

Butterfly

Calcium carbonate

Snails and other mollusks build strong shells out of calcium carbonate.

One deep-sea snail has extra protection—iron sulfide scales, which are like chain mail.

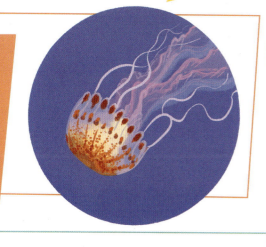

Horseshoe crab

Water

Jellyfish are 95% water. Water pressure gives them shape, and they squirt water out to move.

Pheromones

Some animals communicate through pheromones—chemical messengers that work outside the body.

Ants leave trails of pheromones to lead their workmates to food or warn them of danger.

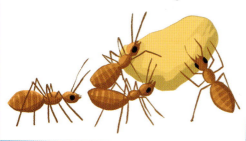

Hormones

Hormones are chemical messengers that help control the body's organs and chemical balance.

One hormone—adrenaline ($C_9H_{13}NO_3$)—makes your heart beat faster, so you can react quickly to danger.

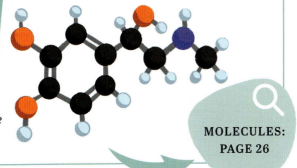

Adrenaline

MOLECULES: PAGE 26

Food chemicals

Food gives us nutrients to build our bodies, grow, and repair damage. Eating the right amounts helps us stay healthy.

The range of foods in a balanced diet gives us all the nutrients we need.

Digestion

Food enters the digestive system (gut), where enzymes break it down into molecules small enough to be absorbed.

ENZYMES: PAGE 74

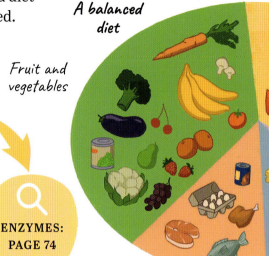

A balanced diet

Fruit and vegetables

Bread, potatoes, pasta, etc

Fatty or sugary food

Dairy products

Meat, fish, eggs, and beans

Liver

Gallbladder

Appendix

Small intestine

Stomach

Pancreas

Large intestine

The small molecules pass through the gut wall and are carried to cells for metabolism.

Healthy diets include carbohydrates, proteins, lipids, vitamins, minerals, fiber, and water.

MORE

Food additives

"Fortified" foods have added vitamins or minerals. Other food additives, including salt, make food look, feel, or taste better, or last longer.

In Europe, E numbers show that food additives have been tested for safety. Curcumin, a natural food dye from turmeric root, is E100.

Turmeric

Curcumin

Carbohydrates

Carbohydrates—sugars and starch—come from foods like potatoes, bread, and pasta. They are broken down into glucose, and excess glucose is stored as fat or glycogen.

Amylase in saliva breaks down starch. Bread tastes sweet if you keep chewing it.

Mouth bacteria turn sugars into tooth-decaying acids—one reason that sugars in carbonated drinks and sweets are unhealthy.

GLUCOSE: PAGE 56

ACIDS AND ALKALIS: PAGE 16

Proteins

We get proteins from meat, nuts, tofu, and eggs.

Protease enzymes break proteins into amino acids, ready to build new proteins.

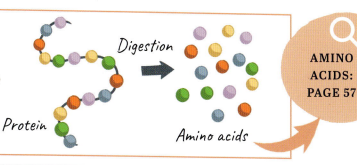

Protein

Digestion

Amino acids

AMINO ACIDS: PAGE 57

Lipids

We get lipids—fats and oils—from vegetable oils and oily fish. We need them for energy and cell membranes, but too much is unhealthy.

Lipase digests fat by snipping the molecules apart.

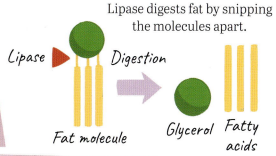

Lipase

Digestion

Fat molecule

Glycerol

Fatty acids

Vitamins

Fruit and vegetables give us many essential vitamins.

Vitamin K, which helps blood clot, is found in green leafy vegetables.

Citrus fruit provides Vitamin C for healthy skin and gums.

Minerals

Nuts and seeds provide minerals, including magnesium, calcium, and iron.

We need iron for hemoglobin, which carries oxygen in the blood.

A hemoglobin molecule contains 10,000 atoms— just four are iron.

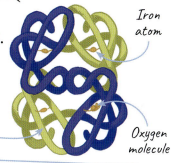

Iron atom

Chain of amino acids

Oxygen molecule

Fiber

We can't digest plant cellulose—we don't have cellulase enzymes—but fruit and vegetables give us fiber, which moves food along the gut.

Water

We need to drink around 6 cups of water a day to keep hydrated.

"Wet" foods also provide water.

WATER: PAGE 66

Chemicals in the home

The chemicals in our houses are often highly processed and engineered to make materials for strong, safe, comfortable homes.

Houses are made of construction materials with the right properties, such as brick walls, glass windows, wooden beams, and good insulation. Composites are materials combined to make them better—steel-reinforced concrete is stronger and more flexible than concrete or steel alone.

MATERIALS AND PROPERTIES: PAGE 14

Sydney Opera House is built with steel-reinforced concrete.

Indoor furnishings are designed for comfort. Household energy arrives through pipes and wires.

Everybody's home is different, but some things are usually there.

Clean water flows in through taps, or faucets—and drains away mixed with dirt, soap, and detergents.

HOME INSULATION: PAGE 83

MORE

How soap works

Soap and detergents are "surfactants"—surface-acting agents. They help water grip dirt by reducing its surface tension.

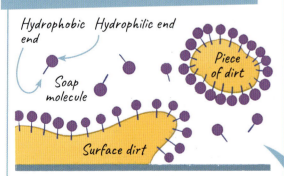

Hydrophobic end   Hydrophilic end

Soap molecule

Piece of dirt

Surface dirt

One end of a soap molecule is hydrophilic (loves water) and dissolves in water. The other end is hydrophobic (hates water) and sticks to the dirt. The soap surrounds small pieces of dirt, so water rinses away the dirt with the soap.

WATER: PAGE 66

Bathroom

Bathrooms are often made of porcelain, glass-reinforced plastic, or plastic-stone composites.

Our toiletries include: soap, shampoo, toothpaste, and antiseptics.

Bleach—a stain-removing, disinfecting solution made of sodium hypochlorite (NaOCl)—is a common cleaner.

Foaming Bleach
TOILET CLEANER

Kitchen

Kitchens have everyday chemicals such as baking soda.

BAKING SODA: PAGE 17

Salt, herbs, and other seasonings make food tastier.

Basil contains estragole ($C_{10}H_{12}O$), also used in perfumes.

Dishwashing liquid and kitchen cleaners tackle greasy surfaces.

FOOD ADDITIVES: PAGE 78

Estragole

CHEMICAL FORMULAE: PAGE 26

Bedroom

Fabrics in our clothes and bedding are made of fibers—either natural ones such as silk, wool, and cotton, or synthetics such as polyamide.

Fabrics are dyed and designed to catch our interest.

POLYAMIDE POLYMERS: PAGE 89

A reflective coating of silver on a mirror shows us the effect of our clothes and cosmetics.

Family room

Our homes are safer because of flame-retardant chemicals, such as aluminum hydroxide.

Clever chemistry makes our devices work. The liquid crystals in LCDs (liquid crystal displays) are molecules with structure like a solid, but they shift in an electric charge.

The molecules line up and tilt, controlling the light filtering through, so the image changes.

Light-emitting diodes (LEDs) in lights, thin-screen televisions, and touch screens are semiconductor devices.

SEMI-CONDUCTORS: PAGE 83

Garage

Cars need other chemicals besides fuel. Antifreeze solution stops the engine from icing up by lowering the freezing point of water.

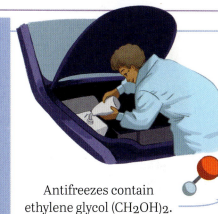

Garage shelves often store garden chemicals.

Antifreezes contain ethylene glycol ($CH_2OH)_2$.

Wood treatments protect fences from weathering.

AGRO-CHEMICALS: PAGE 86

Conductors and insulators

We depend on heat and electricity, but they can be dangerous. Conductors and insulators help us use them safely.

MATERIALS AND PROPERTIES: PAGE 14

Conductivity is the property of how well energy—heat or electricity—flows through a material.

Insulators block the flow. Good **conductors** let it pass through easily.

Heat conduction

In solids, thermal energy (heat) is conducted by particles vibrating.

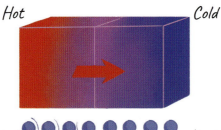

Hot   Cold

Warmer particles vibrate more, passing energy to their neighbors. The heat flows from hot to cold until the heat is evenly spread.

PARTICLE THEORY: PAGE 10

Atoms in hot area lose energy

Atoms in cool area gain energy

Electrical conduction

Electrical conduction is the flow of electrons ("charge") through a material. We harness this energy as electric current, or electricity.

When a current flows, all the free electrons move in one direction.

Metal ion   *Free electron*

Metals have free electrons because of metallic bonds.

METALLIC BONDS: PAGE 29

We live with many insulators, conductors, and semi-conductors.

Copper is used for indoor wiring and the pins on electrical plugs. Aluminum—another excellent conductor—makes cables that carry electricity long distances.

Electricity towers hold up overhead cables.

ELECTRICITY: PAGE 58

MORE

Convection and radiation

Heat transfer in liquids and gases happens by **convection**.

When fluids are heated, the warmer particles move around more, transferring energy to cooler areas. When a pan of water is heated, the particles move in convection currents. Magma does this, too.

Cool molecules sink   *Heated molecules rise*

Objects that aren't touching transfer heat by **radiation**. Heat from the sun reaches Earth through space in solar radiation.

OUR WORLD: PAGE 64

Insulators:

Pan handles and oven gloves
Wooden handles and padded oven gloves insulate us from hot ovens.

Home insulation
Insulating methods block heat loss and save energy in homes.

Loft insulation fiber

Double glazing

Cavity wall insulation foam

CHEMICALS IN THE HOME: PAGE 80

Plastic sockets
Wall sockets and plugs are plastic to protect us from an electric shock from the metal parts.

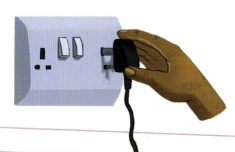

Conductors:

Electric toothbrush
An electric toothbrush's casing is in nonconducting plastic, but there are wire coils hidden inside the handle and the charger base. The toothbrush charges because electricity running through the charger coil produces a magnetic field that induces (creates) a current in the toothbrush coil.

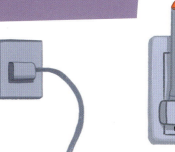

Charging cables
Wires in chargers transfer electricity to a device's battery when it needs more energy.

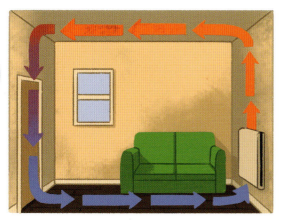

Radiators
Radiators heat mainly by convection. Hot air rises and sets up a convection current where more cool air is heated up.

Semiconductors
Semiconductors are made from semimetals. They are used as "switches" to control the flow of current in our devices.

SEMIMETALS: PAGE 44

Chemistry in medicine

Medicines keep us healthy or make us better when we are ill. They are powerful chemicals and can be harmful if they're not taken properly.

Many modern medicines were originally found in nature. Penicillin, an antibiotic, was first discovered in mold in 1928.

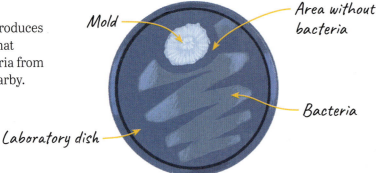

The mold produces penicillin that stops bacteria from growing nearby.

Mold

Area without bacteria

Bacteria

Laboratory dish

Drugs are medicines (pharmaceuticals) and other compounds that affect how our bodies work. They are helpful when we're sick. Drugs taken when we're not sick can be harmful.

PHARMACISTS: PAGE 49

Strong medicines are prescribed by a doctor and supplied by a pharmacist.

Treatments for minor conditions don't need a prescription. They are "over the counter" (OTC) drugs, sold directly to patients.

Drug development

Developing new medicines takes years. Chemists first study compounds in the laboratory and then test formulations in people.

Researchers find out if they are safe, how well they work, and the right dose to give.

Regulators approve new drugs before pharmaceutical companies sell them.

FORMULATIONS: PAGE 52

Drugs are tested in groups of people in clinical phases I, II, and III.

Tens　　Hundreds　　Thousands

| PRECLINICAL | PHASE I | PHASE II | PHASE III |

Some conditions that medicines help are:

Brand names

Companies use brand names to register new drugs. Tylenol, Panadol, and Calpol are all brand names of the painkiller ($C_8H_9NO_2$) called paracetamol in Europe, and acetaminophen in the USA.

CHEMICAL FORMULAE: PAGE 26

Allergies

Pollen up your nose makes you sneeze, because your immune system releases histamine to force it back out. An allergy is the immune system producing too much histamine.

OTC antihistamines treat minor allergies.

Epinephrine is an emergency treatment for serious allergies.

EpiPen Adrenaline (Epinephrine) Auto-Injector 0.3 mg

Cancer

Cancer happens when cells in the body become damaged and grow quickly. Treatments include radiation therapy and chemotherapy.

Fluorouracil ($C_4H_3FN_2O_2$) is a chemotherapy drug that kills cancer cells.

THE HEAVIEST ELEMENTS: PAGE 46

Hormone disorders

Hormones, such as insulin, which controls blood glucose levels, can become unbalanced.

People with diabetes may need to inject insulin.

HORMONES: PAGE 77

Infections

Antibiotics treat bacterial infections, such as pneumonia.

Fever

Very bad cough

Chest pain

Antiviral drugs fight viruses, such as the flu.

Antifungals treat fungal infections, such as athlete's foot.

Vaccines

Our immune system makes proteins called antibodies to fight off infections.

A vaccine gives us a safe part of a virus, such as Covid-19, to get the immune system ready to fight off that virus in the future.

PROTEINS: PAGE 76

Diagnostics

Diagnostic tests, such as X-rays and blood tests, help doctors find out why patients are unwell.

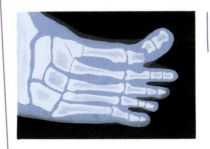

X-rays show broken bones, like this big toe.

Soil and agrochemicals

Farmers and gardeners try to provide the best conditions to grow healthy plants and abundant crops.

Plants need space, oxygen, water, and nutrients from the soil. In nature, they face competition, as well as getting eaten, or being infected by other organisms. To farmers, these are weeds, pests, and diseases. Farmers protect and feed their crops with agrochemicals—pesticides and fertilizers.

Fertilizers

Plants absorb nutrients through their roots. Farmers replace the lost soil nutrients with fertilizers, such as NPK (nitrogen, phosphorus, potassium) fertilizers.

Synthetic fertilizers are effective—they release nutrients quickly—but they can wash out of the soil, causing pollution. Some farming methods, such as monoculture, need more and more fertilizer.

NITROGEN CYCLE: PAGE 72

Various pesticides target different organisms.

Growing one large crop year after year is monoculture.

Pesticides

Farmers control pests to increase their crop yield (growth). Killing pests is effective, but can harm ecosystems. The very toxic insecticide DDT ($C_{14}H_9Cl_5$) accumulated in soil and in the food chain. It killed many birds, and it's now banned in farming.

DDT was used against the Colorado potato beetle.

CHEMICAL FORMULAE: PAGE 26

MORE

Soil

Soil is a mixture of minerals and humus—organic matter.

Sandy soil has large particles and pores, so water and nutrients drain away quickly. Clay soil has small, sticky particles that hold water, which can keep plant roots from getting oxygen. Loam is a good mixture of sand and clay.

MINERALS PAGE 55

Sand   Clay   Loam

Funnel

Water

FILTERING: PAGE 13

pH: PAGE 16

Soil conditioners improve soil properties. The pH of an acidic soil is improved by adding a conditioner containing limestone (calcium carbonate).

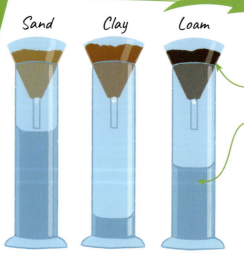

Water filtered through different soil samples

Insecticides

Insects that eat plants include aphids (greenfly), caterpillars, and beetles. They are controlled with insecticides, such as pyrethroids, which mimic plants' natural chemical defenses.

Tunnels of leaf mining fly larvae

 DEFENSE: PAGE 75

Herbicides

Herbicides kill unwanted plants. Some herbicides inhibit (stop) weed growth. Others mimic plant growth hormones—they make weeds grow too fast and die.

AUXINS: PAGE 75

Dandelions are wild flowers or weeds, depending on where they grow.

Molluscicides

Slugs and snails are controlled with molluscicides such as metaldehyde ($C_8H_{16}O_4$).

Fungicides

Microscopic fungi cause diseases such as brown rot, rusts, mildew, leaf spot, and blight. Fungicides contain chemicals such as azoxystrobin ($C_{22}H_{17}N_3O_5$)

Brown rot on apples

Fusarium blight makes cereal grains empty and shrunken.

Natural alternatives

Natural alternatives can be less harmful than synthetic pesticides and fertilizers. Biological control uses the pests' own enemies, such as ladybirds/ladybugs, which eat aphids, or nematodes—microsopic worms—that parasitize mollusks.

Manure—poop—and compost—decayed organic matter—are natural fertilizers that release nutrients slowly.

Worms help break down kitchen compost.

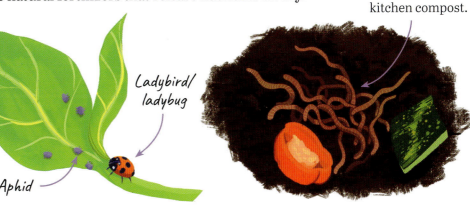

Ladybird/ladybug

Aphid

Polymers

Polymers are amazing molecules. Natural polymers build living bodies, while synthetic polymers—plastics—are used everywhere in the modern world.

Polymers* are long chains of many small molecules (monomers) linked together.

Natural polymers (biopolymers) include cellulose in plants and the DNA in all living things.

Keratin—a protein in hair, nails, and skin—is a biopolymer.

Synthetic polymers are manufactured from monomors produced by cracking fossil fuels.

PROPERTIES: PAGE 14

CELLULOSE: PAGE 74

DNA: PAGE 76

CRACKING: PAGE 51

Different monomors make polymers with very different properties and uses.

Polymerization

Polymerization is the reaction that joins up monomers.

"Addition polymerization" happens when monomers with double carbon-carbon bonds turn the double bond into two single bonds. All the monomers' atoms go into the polymer.

REACTIONS: PAGE 30

SINGLE, DOUBLE, AND TRIPLE BONDS: PAGE 28

Holding both hands is like a double bond.

You let go of one hand to add someone else to the chain.

The polymer of ethene is polyethene (or polyethylene). Polyethene makes polythene bags.

Polyethene is often simply called PE. Its formula is $(C_2H_4)n$. The "n" shows that any number of C_2H_4 units join up in a single PE molecule.

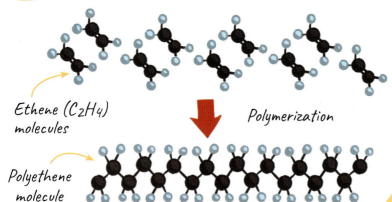

Ethene (C_2H_4) molecules

Polymerization

Polyethene molecule

"Condensation polymerization" is polymerization that links up monomers without breaking a carbon-carbon bond. It often releases water (H_2O) as a by-product. Polyesters are produced by condensation polymerization.

CHEMICAL FORMULAE: PAGE 26

*Poly means "many," and mono means "one."

Polyvinyl chloride (PVC)

PVC is a very strong, hard-wearing plastic, used for water pipes and electrical wiring coatings. Its monomer is vinyl chloride.

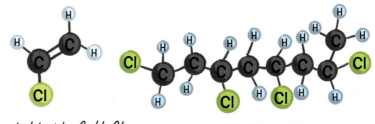

Vinyl chloride, C_2H_3Cl

PVC, $(C_2H_3Cl)_n$

Polyamide (nylon)

Nylon makes strong, flexible fibers. Nylon clothes are soft, lightweight, stretchy, and tough.

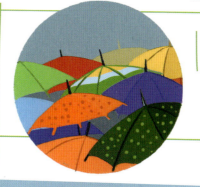

Nylon is waterproofed to make umbrellas.

Polyesters

Polyethylene terephthalate (PET) is the polyester in drinks bottles. It's also used in clothing. Nine bottles can be recycled into one T-shirt!

Elastane

Elastane (spandex), makes strong, stretchy fibers that can adjust their grip as you move.

Synthetic rubber

Synthetic rubber is stretchy, strong, and hard-wearing, with uses from tires to wet suits.

Plastic problems

Polymers last a long time, which means waste plastics hang around for decades. In the oceans, some break down into microplastics—pieces smaller than 5 mm (0.2 in)—which carry toxins into food chains.

Plastics also add to climate change by releasing CO_2 when they are burned.

Even recyclable plastics can be recycled only once or twice.

It helps to find any extra use for them!

Clearing up existing waste, recycling into reusable chemicals, and producing sustainable alternatives are big environmental challenges for plastics.

RECYCLING: PAGE 90

CLIMATE CHANGE: PAGE 70

Energy resources, and recycling

Earth is full of chemical resources and has endless energy from the sun, but people don't always use these things sustainably.

We use natural resources and energy all the time. Captured energy from the sun makes fossil fuels—oil, gas, and coal—which give us electricity, fuels, and chemicals.

Fossil fuels form over millions of years from the ancient remains of plants and animals.

Time

We can't replace them when they're gone, and digging up and burning them causes pollution and global warming.

INDUSTRIAL CHEMISTRY: PAGE 50

CLIMATE CHANGE: PAGE 70

New technologies are making changes in many areas, including:

That's why we need to generate clean (nonpolluting) electricity from renewable sources, and find ways to manufacture and recycle chemicals and products sustainably.*

Scientists are finding amazing solutions to these global challenges.

Renewable Energy

Renewable energy sources can be replaced or are never used up. Power plants already generate some electricity from renewable sources.

Solar cells capture the sun's energy directly. Energy in wind, waves, tides, and waterfalls is captured by rotating turbines that transform moving energy into electricity.

Floating solar panels

Rapeseed

Biomass is wood, organic waste, or crops like rapeseed grown for fuel (biofuel).

CONSERVATION OF ENERGY: PAGE 32

Hydroelectricity is generated from falling water.

Renewable energy isn't perfect. Manufacturing and setting up equipment can harm wildlife habitats. Biomass uses land that could grow food crops, and burning it releases pollutants and greenhouse gases. Not wasting energy is important, wherever it's from.

*"Sustainably" means in ways that help people now and in the future, without harming others or the environment.

Cars

Combustion cars run on gasoline/petrol or diesel fuel. They are being replaced by cleaner vehicles. But electric cars' lithium-ion batteries have a downside—they cause increasing demand for lithium and other metals, and they need electricity for recharging.

Scientists hope to use chitin from crab shells to reduce the metals needed in rechargeable batteries.

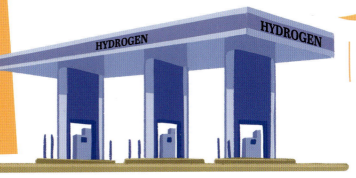

ELECTRO-CHEMISTRY: PAGE 58

Hydrogen-fueled vehicles are also increasing, so hydrogen fueling stations will become more common.

Plastics

New technologies aim to recycle plastic that's currently thrown away.

Pyrolysis—a form of thermal decomposition—breaks down plastics into chemicals, so they can be rebuilt sustainably. In the future, there could be an endless clean recycling loop for all plastics!

Sorting recycling

POLYMERS: PAGE 88

THERMAL DECOMPOSITION: PAGE 31

Water

Some people still don't have enough clean drinking water.

Improved water purification technologies include filtering water through nanopores 3,000 times narrower than a human hair.

Some new desalination plants produce fresh water by mimicking the cell membranes of mangrove trees that grow in salt water.

Mangroves

WATER: PAGE 66

NANO-TECHNOLOGY: PAGE 60

Glossary

ABUNDANT

Plentiful, available in large quantities.

ACID

A chemical with a value lower than 7 on the pH scale.

AGROCHEMICALS

Chemicals used in farming. They include fertilizers and pesticides.

ALCHEMIST

An early scientist who hoped to change substances such as ordinary metals into gold.

ALGAE

Simple organisms that make food using sunlight, similar to plants.

ALKALI

A solution with a value higher than 7 on the pH scale.

ALLOTROPE

Forms of an element, with different arrangements of atoms.

ALLOY

A mixture of a metal with a different element, often another metal.

ANTIBIOTICS

Medicines that kill bacteria.

ATOM

The smallest unit of a chemical element.

ATOMIC NUMBER

The number of protons in an atom. An element's atomic number decides its position on the Periodic Table.

BACTERIA

Very small, single-celled micro-organisms that can be helpful but sometimes act as germs.

BIOCHEMISTRY

The study of the chemistry of living things.

BIOPOLYMERS

Polymers that are produced by living things.

CARBOHYDRATES

Compounds made of carbon, hydrogen, and oxygen atoms, which are found in living things.

CATALYST

A chemical that speeds up a chemical reaction.

CELLS

The tiny units of living things, where metabolism happens.

CHEMICAL BOND

A force that joins atoms together, made by sharing, losing, or gaining electrons.

CHEMICAL REACTION

A process in which atoms are rearranged, changing one or more substances into different substances.

CHLOROPHYLL

A green pigment in plants that absorbs energy from sunlight for photosynthesis.

CLIMATE CHANGE

A long-term change in Earth's average climate patterns and temperatures.

COMPOST

Decayed organic material used as a fertilizer for growing plants.

COMPOUND

A pure chemical made from the atoms of more than one element.

CONDUCTOR

A material that lets heat or electricity pass through it.

CRYSTAL

A solid material where the particles are joined together in a repeating pattern.

DECAY CHAIN - Also called **DECAY SERIES**

The series of elements made when a radioactive isotope decays (falls apart).

DECOMPOSITION

1.When organic waste begins to break down and decay. 2.A chemical reaction in which one compound breaks down into two or more chemicals.

DENSITY

The **space** a substance takes up (its volume) in relation to the amount of matter in the substance (its mass).

DIGESTION

The process of breaking down food to release nutrients in the body.

DISSOLVE

When a solid is mixed with a liquid and it seems to disappear, it has dissolved.

DISTILLATION

A process to separate a mixture of liquids with different boiling points.

DNA

A molecule that carries instructions for the structure and function of living things.

DOPING

Adding a small amount of a substance to a material in order to improve it.

ELECTRON

A negatively charged particle found in an atom.

ELECTRON SHELL

A cloud-like area around an atom's nucleus, where electrons move around.

ELEMENT

A chemical made of a single type of atom. Elements are the simplest chemicals.

ENERGY

The power to do work. It can be changed from one form to another, such as from chemical energy to heat energy.

ENZYME

Biological catalysts that speed up reactions in the body and help break down nutrients.

EQUATION

A way to describe the changes that happen in chemical reactions, using words or formulae.

FERTILIZERS

Fertilizers contain nutrients that plants need to grow. They may be natural or synthetic.

FILTERING

Separating solid particles from a fluid.

FLUID

A substance that can flow. Liquids and gases are fluids.

FORMULAE

Chemical symbols showing the number and type of atoms present in a molecule.

FOSSIL FUELS

Coal, crude oil, and natural gas. They are non-renewable energy sources that add to climate change.

FUNGI

A group of living things that includes mushrooms, molds, and yeast. One is a fungus.

FUNGICIDE

A substance that kills fungi.

GENES

Sequences of chemicals arranged along strands of DNA, which act as coded instructions for cell chemistry.

GRAVITY

A force of attraction that exists between any two masses.

HALF-LIFE

The time taken for half of the nuclei in a radioactive sample to decay.

HORMONE

A biochemical that helps to control bodily processes such as growth.

HYDROCARBON

A molecule containing only carbon and hydrogen atoms.

INORGANIC CHEMICALS

Chemical compounds with molecules that do not contain carbon-hydrogen bonds.

INSULATOR

A material that heat or electricity cannot pass through.

INTESTINES

Tubes inside the gut that extract useful chemicals from food.

ION

An atom that carries an electric charge because it has lost or gained an electron.

ISOTOPES

Forms of an element where the atoms have different numbers of neutrons.

LIPIDS

Nutrients, including fats and oils, made of carbon, hydrogen, and oxygen atoms.

MAGNETISM

A way that a material attracts or repulses another material.

MATERIAL

What a substance is made of, for example, ceramic, metal, or plastic.

MATTER

What everything in the Universe is made of. All matter is made up of tiny particles called atoms.

METABOLISM

The chemical reactions that take place in living cells to keep the organism alive.

METALLOID

An element that sometimes behaves like a metal. A semi-metal.

MICRO-ORGANISM

A living thing that is too small to see with the naked eye.

MINERAL

Naturally occurring inorganic solid with a defined chemical structure.

MOLD/MOULD

A type of fungus that often grows on old food or damp places.

MOLECULE

A group of two or more atoms that are chemically bonded. It is the smallest unit of a compound.

MONOMERS

Small molecules that join together to make polymers.

NANOPARTICLE

A particle no more than 100 nm (0.0001 mm) long or wide. The study and use of nanoparticles is "nanotechnology."

NEUTRON

A particle found in the nucleus of an atom. Neutrons have no charge (neither positive nor negative).

NUCLEUS

1.The centre of an atom. 2.A part inside living cells that contains DNA. The plural is nuclei.

NUTRIENT

Any substance that a living thing needs for energy or growth.

ORGANIC CHEMICALS

Carbon-based compounds. Living bodies are built from organic chemicals.

ORGANISM

A living thing, including plants, animals, fungi, algae, and micro-organisms.

OXIDATION

A reaction in which a chemical gains oxygen atoms.

PESTICIDES

Chemicals used to kill pests, such as insects that eat crops.

pH

A scale to measure the strength of acids and alkalis.

PHOTOSYNTHESIS

A process plants use to produce glucose and oxygen, using water, carbon dioxide, and energy from sunlight.

POLYMER

A very large, chain-like molecule made of repeated smaller molecules called monomers.

PROTEINS

Essential nutrients made of amino acid monomers, which are compounds made of carbon, hydrogen, oxygen, and nitrogen atoms.

PROTON

A positively charged particle found in the nucleus of an atom.

RADIOACTIVE

A radioactive element decays and gives off radiation—small particles of energy.

REACTIVITY

How easily a substance reacts with other substances.

REAGENT

A substance used to test if a chemical reaction has happened.

RECYCLING

The process of reusing something, or turning it into something else.

RESOURCES

Things that can be used, including minerals, fuels, water, and food.

RESPIRATION

The process living things use to release energy from the breakdown of glucose.

SALIVA

A liquid that softens and begins to digest food in the mouth.

SALTS

Compounds produced when acids and alkalis react together.

SEMICONDUCTOR

A material that lets electricity flow through it under some conditions.

SOLUTION

Created when a substance dissolves in a liquid.

STATES OF MATTER

Solid, liquid, or gas. Matter takes a different state, depending on how its molecules are arranged.

SUBATOMIC PARTICLES

Particles inside an atom, including electrons, protons, and neutrons.

SURFACE TENSION

The force that pushes the molecules on the surface of a liquid together.

SYNTHETIC

Human-made, not naturally occurring.

TARNISH

When a metal reacts with oxygen in the air, it goes dull -- it tarnishes.

TOXINS

Poisonous chemicals that can harm living things.

VIRUS

A tiny micro-organism that reproduces inside living cells, often causing illness.

UNIVERSE

All of Space, and all the matter and energy it contains.

VITAMINS

A group of essential nutrients needed in very small amounts for health.

YEAST

A type of single-celled fungus.

Index

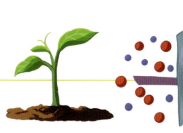
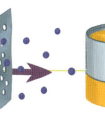